101 Simple Aphorisms for Better Thinking and Living

I0444021

Get Out Of Your Head, It's A Mess In There!

Compiled and Written by Art Dielhenn
Book and Cover Illustrations by Clemmy Le Busque
Foreword by Rick Carson, acclaimed author of Taming Your Gremlin

For My Sons

First published by Ultimate World Publishing 2022
Copyright © 2022 Arthur B. Dielhenn

ISBN

Paperback: 978-1-922828-30-9
Ebook: 978-1-922828-31-6

Arthur B. Dielhenn has asserted his rights under the Copyright, Designs and Patents Act 1988 to be identified as the author of this work. The information in this book is based on the author's experiences and opinions. The publisher specifically disclaims responsibility for any adverse consequences which may result from use of the information contained herein. Permission to use information has been sought by the author. Any breaches will be rectified in further editions of the book.

All rights reserved. No part of this publication may be reproduced, stored in or introduced into a retrieval system, or transmitted in any form, or by any means (electronic, mechanical, photocopying, recording or otherwise) without the prior written permission of the author. Any person who does any unauthorized act in relation to this publication may be liable to criminal prosecution and civil claims for damages. Enquiries should be made through the publisher.

Cover design: Ultimate World Publishing
Cover Illustration: Clemmy Le Busque
Layout and typesetting: Ultimate World Publishing
Editors: Isabelle Russell, Kat Chezim, and Mindi White
Cover image copyright license: garagestock-shutterstock.com

Ultimate World Publishing
Diamond Creek,
Victoria Australia 3089
www.writeabook.com.au

Contents

Foreword 7
Chapter 1: Why I Wrote This Book 9
Chapter 2: Why Read This Book 11
Chapter 3: What Is An Aphorism? 13
Chapter 4: Necessary Stuff 15
Thinking 17
Talking and Listening 39
Action and Achievement 53
Chapter 5: Challenging Stuff 77
Ego, Control, and Attachment 79
Judgment, Blame, and Resentment 105
Fear, Pain, and Worry 121
Chapter 6: Inevitable Stuff 139
Past, Present, and Future 141

CONTENTS

Chapter 7: Good Stuff   145

Relationship and Forgiveness 147

Humility and Acceptance 163

Chapter 8: Sweet Stuff   187

Spirit and Awareness 189

Understanding and Gratitude 203

Chapter 9: More Thinking About Thinking   249

Art Dielhenn   255

Clemmy Le Busque   257

Thanks   259

Library   261

Quotations Tracker   263

Foreword

"Send me a few chapters and I'll be happy to look it over."

This was my response when Art invited me to write a foreword for his new book.

I checked out his webpage. Clearly, this man was sharp as a tack and exceedingly creative. His professional accomplishments were beyond impressive, and he was a gifted "producer" in every sense of the word. What's more, his bio included a photo and he looked like a really nice guy. I looked forward to seeing a few chapters.

In the time between our initial contact and Art's draft arriving, I had unexpected back surgery. When I first looked at what he'd sent, I was in a back brace, in pain, drugged, and mired in the "touch me, I'll bite" blues. My first glance at the manuscript didn't help. I'm not big on platitudes and this book appeared to be filled with them. Worse yet, the platitudes seemed to be harvested from the work of other folks rather than from the author. I laid the manuscript down and I slept for most of the next two days.

FOREWORD

Rested and feeling better, I took a second look at Art's manuscript and was hit smack between the eyes (not for the first time, I fear) with the damage and weirdness of my own snap judgments and preconceived notions.

Truth is, this is a beautifully crafted book filled with wit, wisdom and guidance of the essential sort. Each chapter could be stretched into a book of its own, but, hallelujah, Art chose a far better approach, He simply imparts—with brevity—essential teachings from the work of several human potential pioneers. He then uses illustrative vignettes, many from his own experience, to lend clarity to how each might be applied in daily life.

Savor this book. There is more here than first meets the eye. While it can be a quick read and an enjoyable one at that, I suggest, in addition, an experiential approach. Perhaps select one teaching each morning as your personal growth theme of the day. Keep it in your foreground as you move from one circumstance to the next. Live it. Practice it. Experience it. This material is worth integrating into your being.

I am honored that Art has invited me to write the foreword to this fine work. He has done a beautiful job of providing us a set of guiding principles for a life well lived. I know you will enjoy and benefit from them all.

Live them!

Rick Carson
Taming Your Gremlin

CHAPTER 1

Why I Wrote This Book

I wrote this book as a get-me-through-the-pandemic-with-my-head-screwed-on-straight project.

As a result of the isolation I felt, the isolation many of us felt, I realized that I better double down on my sanity and serenity tools if I was to survive what was coming. And perhaps a good way to do this was to write the book that had been on my mind for a while. Why not? I couldn't binge-watch TV all day.

So, I got together with my friend, Clemmy, and told them I wanted to write a book about all these ideas I had collected and absorbed over the years, but I probably wouldn't write it unless they drew the cartoons.

WHY I WROTE THIS BOOK

(Very cagey and manipulative of me. It would be a hell of a lot of work for them. Surely, they would say no. Then I could use their "no" as an excuse not to write the book while secretly blaming them for my own recalcitrance. Ugh! Sometimes I hate myself.)

But they replied, "YES!" OMG! They said yes! Now I really resented them! Now I really had to do the work and write the damn thing.

So, I started writing and Clemmy started drawing.

CHAPTER 2

Why Read This Book

There is no manual on how to live life. There are lots of suggestions, rules, regulations, guidelines, social norms, religions, laws and many other exterior structures to keep us swimming upstream.

But what about our internal life, the life we live all the time that is not obvious on the outside… our secret place, the one that belongs only to us, where we are most alive, the center of our own beautiful expansiveness? This place is our true self, our intrinsic consciousness that is both fragile and endlessly resilient. It's where we learn and grow, elevate and thrive.

I did not grow up with a manual to guide this internal life. Instead, it was battered and bruised by the chaos and dysfunction surrounding it. My secret place was porous, and consequently dominated by fear, anxiety, pain, doubt, and this weird feeling of never ever being enough, fulfilled, or at peace.

WHY READ THIS BOOK

So, one day my therapist suggested that I might want to do some mindfulness work. I nodded yes but inside dismissed the idea because I actually had no idea what the hell she was talking about. This line from *Blazing Saddles* came to mind, "Badges! We don't need no stinkin' badges!" Mindfulness! I don't need no stinkin' mindfulness.

She was right, of course. Over the ensuing years, I embarked on a journey of inner exploration and was flooded with lots of new ideas, each one its own revelation, its own teaching, its own gift of understanding. Some came from others, some came from books, and many were revealed in the form of slogans, sayings, and aphorisms. I was drawn to the wit and economy of these mini-miracles. They stuck with me, their truthfulness, their humor, and their ease of recall.

It occurred to me, as I started collecting them, that they have been around a very long time, repeated over and over, generation after generation, and have become part of the fabric of life's understanding of itself. They are reminders, prompts, encouragements, sometimes admonitions like "a bird in hand is worth two in the bush" or "look before you leap." Though short, they are mighty, containing deep reservoirs of wisdom.

Spending the last few years writing about these aphorisms has been my way of writing my own inner life manual. I am still the same person I used to be, but my experience of living life has changed forever, shifting from self-absorption to self-awareness, and ultimately to finding some freedom in letting go.

These aphorisms are like cave paintings—they tell our story.

CHAPTER 3

What Is An Aphorism?

An aphorism is a pithy observation that contains a general truth, wisdom, or advice. It may be attributed to a specific person or be a proverb or maxim that has come down through the ages because of its strength in conveying ideas that have "stood the test of time."

Here's an analogy from French cooking that might resonate (thanks, Julia): "When a recipe asks you to reduce a sauce or other liquid, the primary reason is to concentrate the flavors. As water evaporates from the sauce or soup, the flavors of the remaining ingredients concentrate and intensify." — thekitchen.com

An aphorism is like a sauce that has been reduced. Unnecessary words evaporated, leaving behind a brief

WHAT IS AN APHORISM?

well-honed concept reduced to its essence. This essence is concentrated and intensified in its brevity, focus, and general applicability.

CHAPTER 4

Necessary Stuff

Thinking, talking, listening, and action are the human tools we use to get along in the world, to get stuff done. They are so ubiquitous, so prevalent in our daily lives that we take them for granted and don't give them the attention or consideration they rightfully deserve.

They are neutral, the message carriers. For the most part, they are afforded to us throughout our lives. Like tools in a toolbox, they hang around until we are ready to use them. And we use them all the time. How we use these tools defines who and how we are in the world.

Do we use them carelessly, cruelly, and contemptuously or cautiously, cooperatively, and consciously? Do we use them selfishly, greedily, and harmfully, or do we choose to use them with integrity in service of understanding, harmony, and the greater good?

Thinking

*Sometimes my thoughts
just use me for transportation.*

NECESSARY STUFF

The mind is a terrible thing to waste...

THINKING

"The mind is a terrible thing to waste." —United Negro College Fund

The mind is such an amazing concoction of neurons, tissue, memories, ideas, fixations, and on and on and on. It is a powerhouse, creative, productive, logical, insanely capable, and sometimes batshit crazy. For the purpose of this book, I am focusing on the untended, out-of-control mind that makes trouble for us, abuses us, and can even be our own worst enemy.

A new study from Queen's University in Kensington, Ontario, reports that we have about 6200 "thought worms" slithering around in our brains every day. That's a lot of "thought worms" or "thought bundles" crammed into every hour. Yikes!

It's a steady stream, constant and unrelenting. Some thoughts we don't even recognize. Many are positive, constructive, and worthwhile—but what about the rest? What about the thoughts that are injurious, negative, and harmful? What about the hurts, the resentments, the obsessions? What about that pervasive corrosive voice deep inside that abuses and diminishes us?

What is your negative inner voice saying about you?
Are you listening?

NECESSARY STUFF

...It was a table saw, lathe, disk sander, drill press, horizontal boring, router shaper and more. It was a real monster.

THINKING

Power tools are dangerous.
Turn off when not in use.

My dad's hobby was woodworking. In his basement shop he had an all-in-one power tool called a SHOP SMITH. It was huge, heavy, bigger than him, and multi-faceted. It was a table saw, lathe, disk sander, drill press, horizontal bore, router shaper, and more. It was a real monster.

One day, Dad was spinning a four-foot chunk of wood on the lathe to make a new chair leg. I watched with my hands clamped firmly over my ears. The noise was deafening. One second, the leg was whirling and shaping under his chisel, smooth and rhythmic, throwing wood curly cues in the air. The next, the chisel caught a knot and the leg shattered— exploding into hundreds of pieces, hurling fragments and the chisel right over my head to the other end of the basement. Somehow, miraculously, neither of us was injured.

My father turned to me, ashen-faced, and said, "Power tools are really dangerous. Always be careful and always turn them off!"

My brain is the most dangerous power tool I possess. I try to turn it off when not in use.

What do you notice when you don't?

It feels like we are the same person, inseperable, locked in a perpetual boxing match.

THINKING

I am not my thoughts.

Emo Philips once said, "I used to think that the human brain was the most wonderful organ in the body. Then I realized who was telling me this."

There are times when my brain feels like an Itty Bitty Shitty Committee. It's constantly chattering, driving me crazy, scaring me silly, and saying nasty things to hurt me. It feels like we are the same person, that the thoughts are me, inseparable, locked in a perpetual boxing match.

Every thought is true. Every thought has meaning, either good or bad. Every thought is actionable, requiring agreement or disagreement, causing inner strife and turmoil, thought talking to thought about thought thoughtlessly.

It turns out that I am not my thoughts. I am much, much more.

Adyashanti suggested, "If you try to win the war with your mind, you'll be at war forever."

Where do your thoughts end and you begin?

NECESSARY STUFF

THINKING

"A belief is a thought you married."
—Karen Lorre

Thoughts that turn to perceptions that turn to beliefs become entrenched parts of our worldview. They become hardened in our psyche, impenetrable, locked down, and immovable.

Beliefs are a way of sustaining our identity even when they are flawed or cause harm to others or ourselves. Beliefs may also be a misguided way to fathom the unfathomable. We don't understand something, so we insert a belief instead.

Over time, these beliefs become a sacred part of our story, embraced to validate our existence. Some warp our daily experience without permission or conscious awareness. Some beliefs cut us off completely.

It turns out that the mind is like a parachute—it works best when open.

"A wise man changes his mind, a fool never."—Spanish Proverb

What beliefs stifle your wider awareness?

NECESSARY STUFF

What you think about EXPANDS!

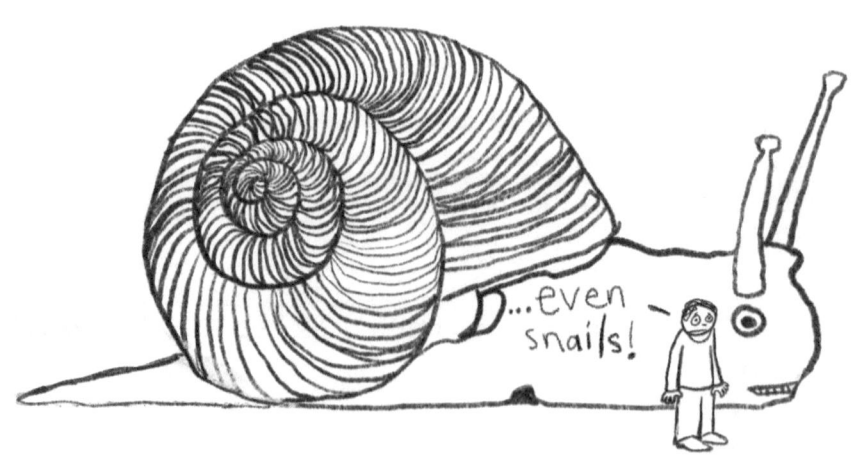
...even snails!

THINKING

"What you think about expands."
—Wayne Dyer

Have you ever noticed how big a little problem gets after obsessing about it for a few days?

Problems are like bread dough. They rise and are very sticky. The more you think about them, the bigger they get, perseverating into palpably pernicious peccadillos. It's hard to fix a problem with the same mind that created it. Usually, that state of mind is stuck.

I love puzzles. Sometimes, pieces fit easily. At other times, they don't. I sit there and I try and I try but nothing, nada, nope. My mind gets clogged and louder as my frustration grows. I can't see the pieces in ways that fit, and the more I try to force the process, the harder it gets.

Then I remember to step away, take a break, and sleep on it. The next morning, when I walk by the puzzle, I see it with an open mind and fresh eyes. One piece after another slips into place with ease.

If you focus on the problem, the problem gets bigger. If you focus on the solution, the solution gets bigger. Sometimes, the solution is a time out.

What do you notice when you stop ruminating about a problem?

Buster charges in that direction, barking furiously. His mind is locked in fury

THINKING

Your mind is an instrument—don't let it play you.

Eckhart Tolle writes, "The mind is a superb instrument if used rightly. Used wrongly, however, it becomes very destructive. To put it more accurately, it is not so much that you use your mind wrongly—you usually don't use it at all. It uses you."

How often have you been in a situation where you were absolutely sure that you were in the right, only to realize later that you were actually in the wrong? How often have you been angry and said things that you needed to apologize for later?

There are times when our emotions get the best of us and our thinking goes haywire. Every time there's a knock at the front door, our dog, Buster, charges ahead, barking feverishly, his mind locked in fury. No amount of reason can deter him. He is driven emotionally by deeply embedded instincts of defense and protection that are out of proportion to the actual threat.

Moments of unreasonable mind that consume us feel absolutely real and valid at the time but are actually skewed by the intensity of our emotional certainty. No matter how confident we feel, we can often be wrong.

"Free will lies in our choice of thought."
—Emmet Fox, The *Sermon on the Mount*

How do you self-regulate in the face of strong emotions?

NECESSARY STUFF

Why, when the truth is obvious, do we continue to buy the lie?

THINKING

> "Most men would rather deny a hard truth than face it."
> —**George R.R. Martin,**
> *A Game of Thrones*

Denial is a defense mechanism; we refuse to accept the reality we are faced with. Sometimes, this stems from stubbornness or pain or ignorance. At other times, denial works to protect us from truths too painful to bear. In the short run, this can be healthy—allowing time to cope with trauma, grief, or pain. But over the long haul, denial sentences us to a persistent alchemy of lopsided perception; often-unconscious mental gymnastics making the world conform to our needs, wants, beliefs, and desires.

Why, when the truth is obvious, do we continue to buy the lie? Why is it so difficult at times to discern the actual truth? How can we so often mistake the person we were meant to be by denying who we really are?

The forces of the universe are so supremely powerful that it is difficult to actually admit our own powerlessness. Sometimes, what we want is more powerful than what is. Eckhart Tolle suggests, "The ego wants to want more than it wants to have." In wanting to want so much, we can trap ourselves in a finely conceived web of deception.

What truth can't you face?

NECESSARY STUFF

what is your
thought life?
where does it
lead you?

come on in, the water's fine!

- 32 -

THINKING

> "Change your thoughts
> and your experience will change."
> —Wayne Dyer

What is your thought life? Where does it lead you? Do you see correlations between your thoughts, feelings, and actions? Does your thought life support or sabotage you? It might be both to varying degrees, depending on your mindfulness and circumstances in that moment.

I didn't think that my thoughts mattered that much. I thought it was actions that mattered most. I didn't feel that I had any control over my thoughts anyway. But it turns out that I do. It takes some practice but thoughts can be chosen, maybe not the first thought but those that follow, if I pay attention. I am now clear that my thought life defines me. It is the raw material that directs my feelings and subsequent actions.

As Emmet Fox suggests in *The Sermon on the Mount*, "What matters to you, truly, is not people or things or conditions in themselves but the thoughts and beliefs you hold concerning them. It is not the conduct of others, but your own thoughts that make or mar you. You write your own history for tomorrow and for next year by the thoughts you entertain today."

What is your thought life?

NECESSARY STUFF

I spend more time with myself than anyone else in the world

THINKING

**"The most important relationship in your life is the relationship you have with yourself."
—Diane Von Furstenberg**

I spend more time with myself than anyone else in the world. So, it's crucial that we (me and my thoughts) get along, that we are kind to each other, support each other, give each other space, and that we don't hurt or pry or make untrue assumptions based on regrets and failures in the past or fears and anxieties of the future.

We are roommates for life. We need to learn how to get along for the long haul. Even when we challenge each other, it's crucial that we understand it's in service to awareness, right-thinking, and productive action.

With this camaraderie comes a sense of self-acceptance, contentment, and peace.

How do you two get along?

NECESSARY STUFF

THINKING

> "You are the sky.
> Everything else—it's just the weather."
> —Pema Chödrön

Here, Pema Chödrön alludes to a higher consciousness separate from the seemingly endless fury of our own thoughts, feelings, emotions, and actions.

Getting there takes some practice. There are many ways to achieve this: spiritual work, meditation, exercise, yoga, contemplation, prayer, walking in the woods, eating ice cream, just sitting quietly for a bit—to name a few. The one key ingredient is that you want it, yearn for it, seek it, and take the necessary steps to find your way there. It's a worthy journey.

In this space, we can pause and feel our true self in the moment. We can see the turmoil below but separate from it by choosing not to engage. In this space, we're able to practice mindfulness, or more aptly, mind emptiness.

It's a clearer, more peaceful view above the clouds. As Eckhart Tolle said, "All the things that truly matter—beauty, love, creativity, joy, inner peace—arise from beyond the mind."

Where is your sky?

Talking and Listening

*If I don't open my mouth,
I can't put my foot in it.*

NECESSARY STUFF

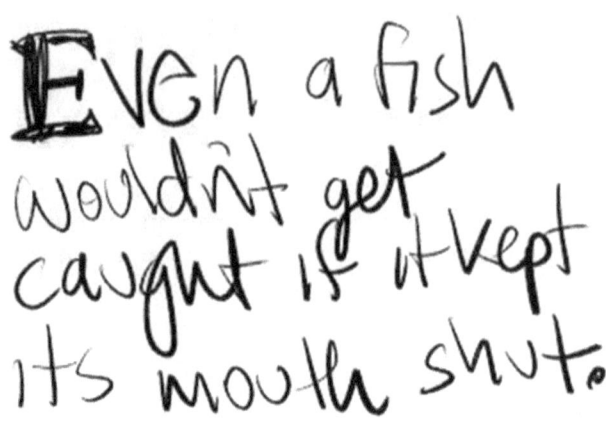

TALKING AND LISTENING

Even a fish wouldn't get caught if it kept its mouth shut.

If I watch my feet as they leave the room, my mouth will surely follow.

Why do we speak? Sometimes, it's for the joy of sharing life experience or communicating necessary information. It can also be for connection or to express our love for one another.

But at other times, we speak to convince, control, defend, argue, accuse, or just overcome the discomfort of silence. The words choke us and must be expelled.

Our impulses can get the best of us, causing us to blurt out things we shouldn't. Sometimes we speak because we're nervous. Sometimes we have no idea why we're speaking.

Mahatma Gandhi was known to say, "Speak only if it improves the silence."

What is the value of silence for you?

NECESSARY STUFF

Sometimes I get lazy and my mouth runs away with itself

TALKING AND LISTENING

Say what you mean, mean what you say. Just don't say it mean.

"Be careful of your thoughts. They may become words at any moment."—Iara Gassen

There are times when I get lazy and my mouth runs away with itself. In those instances, I realize that I am not paying attention and some other part of me is expressing itself, a part unknown to me, a part not fully in my grasp.

Maybe I'm speaking through burdens or hurts from the past. Sometimes fear or anger or resentment drive my mouth. If I have nothing loving, helpful, constructive, or understanding to say, it's best not to say anything at all.

As the Sufi poet, Rumi, once said, "Before speaking, let your words pass through three gates:

- Is it true?
- Is it necessary?
- Is it kind?"

Don Miguel Ruiz, in his first agreement, suggests, "Be impeccable with your word. Speak with integrity. Say only what you mean. Avoid using the word to speak against yourself or to gossip about others. Use the power of your word in the direction of truth and love."

How are you not impeccable with your words?

NECESSARY STUFF

Wait, why am I talking?
—David Emerald

Have you ever *not* been able to stop talking? Have you ever felt so compelled to speak that you didn't care about the consequences?

Your observer-self says, "STOP TALKING! You're just digging yourself a deeper hole."

But due to nervousness, ego, hubris, fear, or pride, you still can't stop. You just have to say what you have to say. Damn the torpedoes; full speed ahead.

Conversely, have you ever been on the other side of a rant like that? Perhaps when you are on the phone with someone who rattles on incessantly and every time you try to get a word in edgeways, the person raises their voice and talks right over you, hijacking the conversation. All you want to do is hang up. So, trying to be polite you tell the person you need to get off. The person says, "Okay," then launches into yet another unstoppable diatribe.

Sometimes, we are so desperate to connect that it feels impossible to disconnect. Then we must ask ourselves The question posed by Scott Howard, "Why am I still talking?" or its acronym, WAIST.

What are you feeling when driven to rant?

NECESSARY STUFF

TALKING AND LISTENING

"Learn to listen, listen to learn."
—Roni S. Lebauer

There's an old actor joke that goes something like this: bullshit bullshit my line. Bullshit bullshit my line. Sadly, many of us listen this way, dominated by our own agendas, feelings, and thoughts. The fine art of listening, without judgment or agenda, is a spiritual act of great magnitude. It often eludes us.

How do you listen?

Are you anxious to justify, interpret, argue, convince, control, defend, or explain? Are you desperate to make your own point? Do you remember a person's name when introduced, or do you forget it right away because you're so consumed with what you want to say next?

So, often we find it hard to listen because we are driven to articulate our own version of the world. It takes practice, self-discipline, and great self-esteem to listen. We have to set ourselves aside and sit in the space of nothing to defend, nothing to prove, nothing to want. Only then is real listening possible. How else could I ever learn how much I didn't know?

Try spending a whole day just listening to the rhythms of your own heart and the hearts of others.

What do you notice when you do?

NECESSARY STUFF

TALKING AND LISTENING

Self speaks first and speaks the loudest.

Sometimes, all I can hear is my own inner voice shouting at me. It's so loud, a constant closed feedback loop, uninviting, protecting, and unaware of everything except the endless drone of its own nonsense.

My youngest son, in a moment of anger, shouted at me, "You have no idea who I am." He later retracted this statement but I knew he spoke truth. Did I really know him or only know who I wanted him to be? I was actually shocked by my own projections, how little I was seeing him, his essence, his unique beauty, as being separate from any imagining I might have about him. How could I love him so much and know him so little. Was I doing this with everyone in my life?

At the age of twelve, this son taught me one of the greatest lessons of my life: to put myself aside and truly listen, stand in his shoes and come from a place of curiosity devoid of self-interest, defensiveness, or judgment.

After that, we made a pact. We decided to share details of our lives unknown to the other, fears we had, music we liked, stuff we learned, and things that happened. Often these conversations took place in the car going to or coming from. Each an absolute treasure.

What happens when you really set yourself aside?

NECESSARY STUFF

TALKING AND LISTENING

> **"It's okay to cross the street
> to avoid making small talk."
> —Susan Cain**

In her book *Quiet: The Power of Introverts in a World that Can't Stop Talking,* Susan Cain argues that when we moved from an agrarian to an industrial society, opening one's mouth became highly monetizable, leaving quiet introspection behind, devalued, even pathologized. We moved from planting and growing to building and selling.

Selling requires a huge marketing megaphone that never stops spewing.

We discussed earlier that we have in excess of 6200 "thought worms" every single day. Well, can you begin to imagine how many external messages assault us per day? How many opinions, points of view, political and/or religious rants, emails, texts, and advertisements?

Our lives are so inundated by these endless and relentless messages that we yearn for quiet introspection.

It feels good just saying it: quiet introspection.

How do you find peace and quiet?

Action and Achievement

Do the thing you think you can't do.

NECESSARY STUFF

ACTION AND ACHIEVEMENT

"It's easier to act your way into a new way of thinking than think your way into a new way of acting."
—Jerry Sternen

Okay, here's an oldie but a goodie. Three frogs are sitting on a log, and one decides to jump off. How many are left? Two? No, three. Bert only *decided* to jump, He didn't actually do it.

Honestly, he probably talked himself out of it. "I bet the water is freezing. I know I have to get to work but it's so cozy sitting in the sun on this log and that lily pad looks so dang far away! And besides, I don't want to leave my friends."

We are all subject to "I shoulds" or "I ought tos." But none, absolutely none of this thinking gets us off the log/couch. The best-laid plans do exactly that, they lie there like wet noodles unless they are implemented with systematic action, bringing about a productive satisfying result.

Actions speak louder than words, thoughts, intentions, decisions, or dreams.

What action have you been wanting to take but haven't?

NECESSARY STUFF

ACTION AND ACHIEVEMENT

The dream *is* the journey.

According to Oxford Languages, a dream can be "a cherished aspiration, ambition, or ideal" and simultaneously "an unrealistic or self-deluding fantasy."

A dream is a thing, a noun. It's not active. "To dream" is active, a verb. We do it at night in our sleep but if we are dreaming during the day, we might be accused of being a "sluggard, a mope, negligent, misty, dim, indistinct, or cloudy."
—Milton Katselas, *Dreams Into Action*

Kobe Bryant was a great basketball player with limitless potential. He could have settled and ridden his talent to the sports stratosphere but he wanted more. He wanted to be the best, so he worked at it tirelessly every single day. His commitment to his craft was legendary. For him, the dream wasn't just being the best. The dream was the work, passion, and love he invested in the journey of being the best.

In a public message, Kobe Bryant said, "That's the dream. It's not the destination, it's the journey." For him the dream wasn't the finish line. It was the elevation of his commitment to and engagement in the journey.

What dream yearns for your relentless pursuit?

NECESSARY STUFF

ACTION AND ACHIEVEMENT

There is nothing quite like accomplishing something you once thought out of reach.

The measure of your commitment to any objective is your desire minus your resistance. Do what is intimidating. Feed off the energy of doing the uncomfortable. Focus on getting better, doing better. Don't stand pat.

When I was in seventh grade, I was diagnosed with dyslexia. Words and numbers were a complete jumble. I read at a snail's pace and comprehended little. I did horribly in school and even worse on standardized tests. I stayed back. It was humiliating.

Thanks to my mom's persistence, I worked with a tutor for two years and started to rewire my scrambled brain developing new neural pathways. I finished high school and college (somehow), had a thirty-year career, and took some writing classes. The last thing I ever thought I would do is write anything, much less a book. (Admittedly, these are small bites with lots of quotes and cartoons.) But hallelujah, here it is!

The wondrous magic of life is that we can overcome our resistance and many of our limitations, both real and imagined. We can learn to adapt, be flexible, and grow.

Where are you growing?

NECESSARY STUFF

ACTION AND ACHIEVEMENT

When you're behind, slow down; you'll get there twice as fast.

This is the parable of the tortoise and the hare. It seems counter-intuitive. When behind, speed up! It's common sense. If you're late for an appointment, speed up. If you have a deadline, speed up. After all, it's a-get-on-to-the-next-thing-as-fast-as-you-can-world. Hurry, hurry, hurry. Everything's always going so damn fast that we have to go faster to stay ahead or, God forbid, fall behind.

Here's the fallacy in that notion: Speeding up creates a breeding ground for unforced errors, mistakes, accidents, and a whole slew of potential negative consequences that can forever alter your life. Much of this urgency seems to be self-imposed, causing nothing but undue stress and anxiety. Haste makes waste.

Plus, we miss so much along the way, not the least of which is smelling the roses. Years ago, I went on a bike tour around the Big Island of Hawaii. On the fourth day, we rode fifty miles in the pouring rain. I'm talking cats and dogs pouring. I was freezing, fingers numb, by the side of the road fixing a flat tire when my eye caught a bus passing by. All the passengers looked down at me, pity in their eyes for my soaking cold predicament. I couldn't help but feel sorry for them trapped in that bus while I was ankle-deep in the mud having the time of my life.

"There is more to life than increasing its speed."—Gandhi

What is the value of hastening slowly?

NECESSARY STUFF

ACTION AND ACHIEVEMENT

Hard by the yard, a cinch by the inch.

How do you eat an elephant, all at once or a bite at a time? Obvious, right?

This is one problem with goals: they are often too big and more like fantasies or dreams. They lack substance in reality. A goal is usually a result, not an action. Goals lack the attention to detail, strategic thinking, and planning that actually makes them possible in the real world.

Implementation takes time, energy, and resources to bring a goal to fruition.

My dad used to tell me, "Do little things well and bigger things will come asking to be done."

When have you accomplished something of real value in your life? I bet it didn't happen overnight. It happened with due deliberation and hard work, day in and day out. I have to constantly remind myself that life is no different. I must be patient and let it come to me as I lend myself to it—kindly and lovingly with deep forgiveness and appreciation.

What's your next bite?

NECESSARY STUFF

ACTION AND ACHIEVEMENT

Act now.
Procrastinate later.

NO! I DON'T WANNA!

Procrastination is the heartbeat of instability, creating chaos both internally and externally. It can be driven by the fear of doing, saying, or asking for what you need or want. Sometimes it's the fear of failure. There is much unmanageability in procrastination. The mind is very comfortable with becoming something tomorrow. Sadly, the long-term results can be devastating.

Life's needs can be suppressed, repressed, or flat-out denied, creating a huge traffic jam deep inside that exacts a huge psychological and emotional toll. The more I procrastinate, the more things are left undone or unresolved, the more anxious I get, producing more dysfunction, stress, and paralysis dragging me into a swamp of self-loathing.

After procrastinating for far too long, I become disgusted with myself, not to mention angry. The anger fuels my intention to complete all the crap I've been avoiding. So, I get to work and before I know it, eureka! It's done and I feel better, I feel lighter, I feel freer. I wonder why it took me so long, driving myself crazy in the process.

Courage in action is one of life's true measures.

When you procrastinate, what's really going on?

NECESSARY STUFF

ACTION AND ACHIEVEMENT

"Don't just do something, sit there."
—Sylvia Boorstein

Sometimes the best action is no action at all. When in doubt, sit it out. This is a choice—to pause and examine our motives. Are we getting into other people's business? Are we trying to control the uncontrollable? Are we trying to force tomorrow's work today?

Many are driven to be in motion all the time, constantly doing, doing, and doing more. Sometimes, we are so driven to activity that we ignore our own needs, our own health, our own peace of mind. At these times in my life, I've realized I was often running from or chasing after something—hiding, fearful, or distracting myself, afraid to slow down and really acknowledge the truth in my life at that moment.

For better or for worse, the moment is all we have. Sometimes, it's uncomfortable, sometimes wonderful. While setting aside time to experience it might feel awkward or wasteful, sometimes it's the correct action to take.

Blaise Pascal wrote, "All men's miseries derive from not being able to sit in a quiet room alone."

What do you notice when you do?

NECESSARY STUFF

ACTION AND ACHIEVEMENT

HALT
National Center for Biotechnology Information

Pause when agitated. Don't text when upset. Think before you hit send. Put that angry email in the drafts folder. Don't retaliate. You will only have to apologize later. Take a beat and, as Ice Cube rapped, "Check yourself before you wreck yourself."

Often, the best letter written is the letter best unsent.

Take an inventory of your physical and emotional state. Utilize the acronym HALT: Hungry, Angry, Lonely, Tired. If you are experiencing any of these conditions, address them immediately. If you don't, any one of them might adversely affect your subsequent interactions.

When babies cry or throw a temper tantrum, they are either tired, hungry, wanting attention, or in need of a diaper change. Honestly, I don't think adults are much different. Sure, we're supposed to be grown up but we still have all those needs. Our advantage is that we can pause, take a moment, identify what's wrong, and make course corrections that are needed to avoid the storm.

How could you use HALT?

NECESSARY STUFF

ACTION AND ACHIEVEMENT

What you resist persists.
It just gets louder and more distorted.

Many of us embody two lives—the life we live and the life we resist. The measure of our commitment to a goal is our desire minus our resistance. As I write this paragraph, I can feel a tug of resistance weighing me down. I'm not sure what I want to say. The more I resist, the harder the task seems, the more my resistance persists.

How do I deal with this resistance? I could stop altogether, but I don't want to stop. So, I might as well accept the resistance and start writing anyway. I'll just see what happens.

Sometimes, I get into bed and resist sleep. My brain is whirling around and sleep seems miles away. At that moment I notice that I am holding myself tightly and I make a mental note to relax my body from head to toe. Just like magic, my body melts into the mattress. I can feel my mind starting to embrace the idea that it is time for sleep. I can worry, obsess, argue, and problem-solve tomorrow. I accept these thoughts and let go again, because my body forgot to stay relaxed. I do this back and forth a few times, quietly in rhythm, then wake up the next morning.

Where is the friction in your life? What are you resisting right this second? Is it a person, place, thing, or situation?

How is acceptance the flip side of resistance?

NECESSARY STUFF

ACTION AND ACHIEVEMENT

Progress not perfection: do an adequate job at a moderate pace.

Take it easy. Perfectionism is an illusion and a trap. It is also one of the many tools used by Mr. Procrastination. He says, "Well, if you can't get it right or make it perfect, don't even bother!"

Perfectionism stops us from accomplishing great things. Those willing to proceed occasionally make mistakes and fail. Sometimes even fail miserably. They are the ones who confront their own obstacles, both real and imagined, who persevere, and are most likely to succeed.

I remember when I started my career. I wanted everything to go perfectly. I was petrified of making mistakes. Needing help sorting out my fears on the matter, I sought guidance from my therapist. As we were winding down the session, he asked, "How many mistakes will you allow yourself per day?"

This sounded like a legitimate question, so I responded, "One or two?"

He couldn't stop laughing!

How does perfection hobble your progress?

NECESSARY STUFF

Smart, what do you mean, "smart"?

S.M.A.R.T.
George Doran, Arthur Miller, and James Cunningham

S = Specific
M = Measurable
A = Attainable
R = Realistic
T = Timely

Have you ever tried to succeed without a plan? How did it go? As the saying goes, "Failing to plan is planning to fail!"

When setting out to accomplish something it's advisable to create a structure for your intention. The SMART acronym gives the targeted objective a realistic structure to progress consistently over time. Much like blueprints for a building, engineering plans for a bridge, a new design for a car, a will for your kids, or having a heart-to-heart with a loved one.

Everything that is built, created, manufactured, or designed requires some kind of plan, a roadmap to follow to completion.

Many feel that this type of regimentation stifles creativity. "It's not my style. I'm just going to wing it." This response is understandable. Freedom and intuition are great strengths of the creative mind. When starting in the creative phase it's important not to be bogged down in reality. That's how we think creatively out of the box.

But the creative phase (the idea) is followed by the implementation phase (the how of the follow through) and this phase requires structure for efficient execution.

What plan are you working on?

CHAPTER 5

Challenging Stuff

Here's where things can get tricky and sticky. Herodotus suggests, "Of all men's miseries, the bitterest is this: to know so much and have control over nothing."

Herodotus was a Greek historian born 484 years before Christ. Even back then, he knew that no matter how smart, educated, powerful, or ingenious we are, we can't possibly predict the future. If we could, it wouldn't be called the future. It would be called the present.

Yet, day after day, most of us try to defy our own powerlessness by trying to control, manipulate, change, or alter our life's trajectory or the trajectory of others lives.

The following are some tools we use to that end!

Ego, Control, and Attachment

*If you think you're the smartest one
in the room, you're in the wrong room.*

CHALLENGING STUFF

Learning to manage your gremlins is one of life's great accomplishments

EGO, CONTROL, AND ATTACHMENT

> ## "Don't think less of yourself, just think of yourself less."
> —Ken Blanchard

This one reminds me of the quote by Groucho Marx: "I don't want to belong to any club that will accept me as a member."

For many of us, there are times when we don't think much of ourselves. For some, these thoughts are constant and unrelenting, disturbing our well-being and undermining our sense of self-worth. It's like an abusive tormenting voice in our head. Rick Carson calls it the *gremlin*.

"Your gremlin is the narrator in your head. He wants you to accept his interpretations as reality, and his goal, moment to moment, day to day, is to squelch the natural vibrant you within. He is intent on making you miserable."
—Rick Carson, *Taming Your Gremlin*

Your gremlin could be a he, she, or it. It could also be a chorus of voices spewing idea fragments and clogging your soul with recrimination, self-loathing, and fear.

Managing your gremlins is a heroic accomplishment.

What nasty things does your gremlin say about you?
Are you tired of listening?

CHALLENGING STUFF

EGO, CONTROL, AND ATTACHMENT

Don't roam the world
with a broken heart.

Someone once advised me, "Stop wearing your life like a rash."

I didn't understand what he meant. Not much of a surprise. I didn't understand myself.

I wasn't comfortable in my own skin. It felt itchy, even painful at times. I felt awkward, as if I was two different people living parallel lives. On the outside, I was successful, competent, and thriving. Inside, I was lost, confused, sad, angry, and isolated. It seemed impossible to reconcile these two ways of being.

Sometimes, there are crossroads we come to where we either reject life or love it unconditionally, seeking reconciliation in the process.

Arthur Rubenstein said, "I've found that if you love life, life will love you back."

In choosing to make peace with life, and myself, I chose to love myself in it, to draw on my own intrinsic self-worth. No one and nothing can take it from me. It's who I really am. I might forget at times, but in remembering I can always reclaim it, finding myself anew.

Every aphorism in this book represents a lesson that I have been gifted on my journey. Today I like myself much better than any of the people I used to be. Thankfully, I don't itch or scratch much anymore.

What would you like to reconcile?

CHALLENGING STUFF

If I do enough, accomplish enough and acquire enough, I will be happy...

EGO, CONTROL, AND ATTACHMENT

"You can only lose what you cling to."
—Buddha

We spend much of our life chasing attachments—people, ideas, beliefs, objects, jobs, memories, expectations, resentments—a whole host of connections woven into the fabric of our life experience.

Most of these attachments are generated by our need for outside validation, for love, for security, for comfort.

I thought, "If I do enough, accomplish enough, and acquire enough, then I will be happy, content, and complete." For some reason, I was never enough as I was. The attachments compensated for my feelings of inadequacy and insufficiency.

But regrettably, they never ultimately satisfied me. How could they? Often fleeting, they always left me wanting more.

"The ego wants to want more than it wants to have. And so the shallow satisfaction of having is always replaced by more wanting. This is the psychological need for more, that is to say, more things to identify with. It is an addictive need, not an authentic one."
—Eckhart Tolle, *A New Earth*

What attachments do you bear unwillingly?

CHALLENGING STUFF

EGO, CONTROL, AND ATTACHMENT

All I ever wanted was an unfair advantage.

The hubris of entitlement is an astounding thing to behold. Its arrogance is especially noxious when practiced by the rich, the famous, and the powerful. Let's face it, they already have an edge. Sadly, for everyone else, many of them are never satisfied and always want more.

Emmet Fox suggests in his work *The Sermon on the Mount* that misdirected entitlement in any walk of life offers "temptations . . . for self-glory and self-aggrandizement . . . for personal honors and distinctions, even for material gain; temptations to allow personal preferences to hold sway in our counsels when it is a sacred duty to deal with all men in perfect impartiality." Hmmmmm.

But even we normal folks can experience entitlement at times. It can make us feel on top of the world—invincible. We feel it when we are having a run of good luck, when we are flush and expecting more, when our beliefs outpace our common sense and humanity, when we are sure we are right and everyone else wrong, when our ego swells in the delusion of our own self-importance.

We live in a "win at any cost" culture where humility is overshadowed by greed and the idea of "self-will run riot," lacking real purpose and meaning. We can actually lose ourselves in this environment and find ourselves unable to identify the person we are meant to be.

How can you stay right-sized?

CHALLENGING STUFF

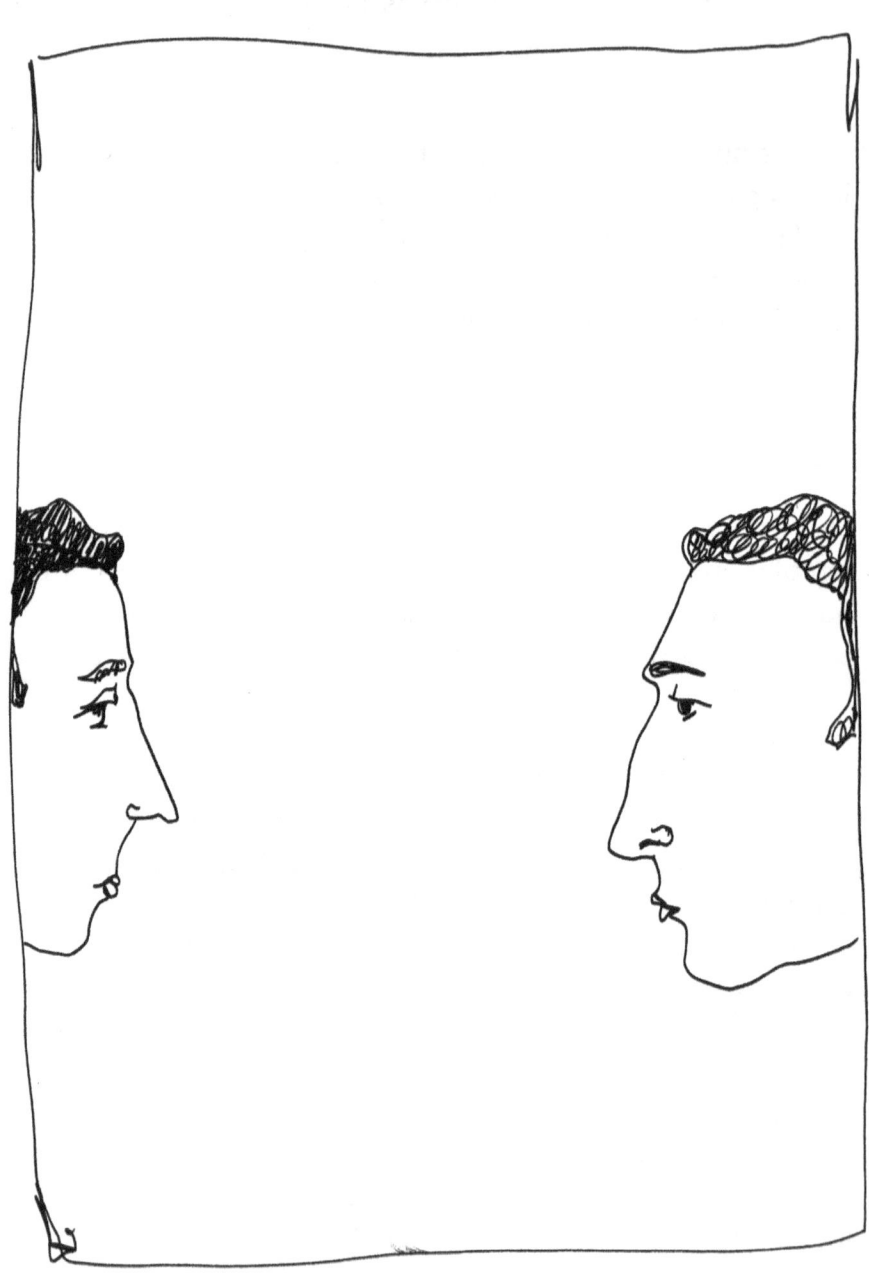

EGO, CONTROL, AND ATTACHMENT

My ego is not my amigo.

"We don't see things as they are. We see them as we are."
—Anais Nin

My ego is the filter through which me, myself, and I assimilate the world around us. My ego asserts my right to be. It can be both defensive and offensive, constantly fighting tooth and nail for dominance or survival, and it doesn't take prisoners.

Oops, actually it does: ME! It's hard to see the world as it is when I view it through the lens of who I think I am or who I think I ought to be.

Sometimes, my ego's grandiosity knows no bounds. The most disturbing part of this phenomenon is that my ego is a chameleon hiding in the folds of its own self-denial while simultaneously purporting to be successful, altruistic, and generally ecstatically wonderful.

Epictetus noted, "It is impossible to begin to learn that which one thinks one already knows."

Since my ego's tendencies are so formidable, it's hard to change what I can't acknowledge. At times, it takes all my will to surrender my will.

What do you notice when you right-size your ego?

CHALLENGING STUFF

EGO, CONTROL, AND ATTACHMENT

> **Assumption is presumption,**
> **the breeding ground for dysfunction.**
> *— The Four Agreements*

Don Miguel Ruiz, in his third agreement, states, "Don't make assumptions. Find the courage to ask questions and to express what you really want. Communicate with others as clearly as you can to avoid misunderstandings, sadness, and drama. With just this one agreement, you can completely transform your life."

To make assumptions is to presume that we know the nature of another's heart, mind, and spirit. Our assumptions rob them of their absolutely unique humanity and they rob us of knowing them as they truly are.

It has been said that listening is love. Listening is a great acknowledgment of another. Only then can we respond with some degree of real union. If we are making assumptions, then once again our ego is talking to itself and the other is just a prop in the conversation, viewed but not seen.

What is the arrogance in assumption?

CHALLENGING STUFF

EGO, CONTROL, AND ATTACHMENT

Others may resent you doing for them what they can't do for themselves.

Oscar Wilde sardonically warned, "No good deed goes unpunished."

My brother was epileptic and suffered greatly from mental illness. He always called for money when he was in a jam. I, of course, feeling guilt and shame that I had some success as he struggled, sent it to him on a regular basis. Then days later he would call raging, angry, and accusatory.

I wrote it off as the ups and downs of his illness. Perhaps it was, in part. I later came to realize that taking the money must have embarrassed him. He may have felt guilty needing me to do for him what he could not do for himself. He may have been grateful and resentful at the same time.

It was selfish on my part. I infantilized him. I was attached to fixing him and his world. I was meddlesome. I gave him money and support hoping that he would get better. I had an agenda. If he got better, I would feel better. I know now that my help came at a great cost to him: the cost of his self-respect, independence, and the ability to make his own way through his own dignified autonomous choices.

How can helping others also be a secret sin of pride?

CHALLENGING STUFF

EGO, CONTROL, AND ATTACHMENT

Helpfulness is the friendly face of control.

Helping an old lady cross the street is deemed a nice gesture. If she didn't ask for help, it's called kidnapping.

If I insist on helping without being asked, it implies that I think you are not capable, that I secretly know better, that, in a very subtle way, I am here to rescue you. It's presumptuous of me to guess or project what you need based on my own worldview. My helpfulness can actually be disempowering.

After careful consideration of my motives, I have to admit that my desire to help or rescue is often based on my need to be needed, my need to control, or my need to feel important.

Are your helpful efforts truly altruistic or do you secretly yearn for something, often unexpressed, in return?

What is the value of waiting for the question?

CHALLENGING STUFF

...I am RIGHT! — And that's THAT!!

EGO, CONTROL, AND ATTACHMENT

I can be right or I can be happy.

Oh boy! This is a biggie. Right? When *being* right is more important than *doing* right, it's hard to see *what is* right.

For a long time, I was the happiest unhappy guy around. I had to be right! When I was determined to be right, the desire to dominate infected me and happiness was irrelevant! Of course, I'm right! How can you not see that?

Of course, it's only my perspective that seems right—my ego's warped perception of the truth. What about the other folks in the room? What about their perspectives? Don't they have equal rights to be right, or wrong?

What if I'm wrong, not right? What's the right thing to do? Admit that I'm wrong, right?

The bottom line is: I'm a lot happier when I don't have to be right, when I can live in acceptance of what is without assigning arbitrary values one way or the other.

Werner Erhard proclaimed, "Happiness is a function of accepting what is."

What do you notice when you have to be right?

CHALLENGING STUFF

EGO, CONTROL, AND ATTACHMENT

If it ain't broke, don't fix it.

My ego wants me to be all things to all people. He's joking, right? First, he wants me to fix you and your stuff, then, time permitting, the old ego might deign to fix some of me and my stuff.

Well, Mr. Fix-It needs to be retired. Mr. Fix-It is afflicted with hubris of monumental grandiosity. He wants to be significant, recognized, and celebrated. He is especially gifted at giving unsolicited advice and has legendary powers when it comes to knowing your needs. He is humble, yet secretly yearns to be world-famous.

Mr. Fix-It is deluded by the intensity of his need to be needed and his desire to control the world around him. He is blinded by his effect on others, imagining that everything he does comes from a heartfelt place of kindness and service.

While trying to force a solution, Mr. Fix-It often intensifies the problem.

How do you feel when Mr. Fix-It tries to fix you?

CHALLENGING STUFF

"facebook is loaded with keyboard warrior wannabe fake fucktards who lack real-life contribotion to a broken society and vent on a fucking computer screen while wacking off to sexy friend's profile pics!"

EGO, CONTROL, AND ATTACHMENT

There are two kinds of business: my business and none of my business.

Imagine a road with one lane on each side. There is a lot of traffic going both ways. Further imagine yourself driving every car in sight on both sides of the street at the same time. What do you think that would be like?

Overwhelming and totally out of control with lots of accidents?

Now, release that image and imagine that each car is driven by its owner and your only responsibility is to drive your own car safely. That's a whole different picture.

The moral of this story is that it's best if we stay on our side of the street and pay attention to our own business while letting others pay attention to theirs.

This, admittedly, is not easy, but the calculus of running one's life while trying to run the lives of others is impossibly complex and often does not end well. I'm a much happier camper when I stay on my side of the street and wish you well on yours.

How can you stay on your side of the street?

CHALLENGING STUFF

I'm so lonely without you, it's as if you were here!

EGO, CONTROL, AND ATTACHMENT

Detach with love.
What!? Really?

Detaching is a way of separating the sticky emotional glue that keeps us stuck in unhealthy relationships or situations. Life is change; attaching and detaching constantly from people, places, things, and situations. We are always in motion and so is everyone else. This coming and going is natural but it can often be punctuated by sadness, anger, embarrassment, disappointment, or regret.

Detachment by its very nature seems like a rupture—explosive, wrenching apart, leaving wreckage in its wake that will have to be atoned for later, if at all. Imagine a multistage rocket detaching from its parts as they are expended, no longer valued, a drag on its trajectory.

It takes practice to detach with love, to accept both the good and the bad and choose not to carry wounds, inflate, inflict, or internalize them. To leave a place, remembering it fondly, even if difficult things happened there. To part from an awful situation, but see the growth in it. To separate from a dysfunctional relationship by setting strong boundaries or leaving altogether and still caring for that person in new ways, wishing them only the best.

It doesn't matter which path you take as long as you take it with love.

How do you detach?

Judgment, Blame, and Resentment

When we give up our needs,
we gain resentments.

CHALLENGING STUFF

JUDGMENT, BLAME, AND RESENTMENT

Blame thrower

Have you ever known someone who blames everything on everybody else, taking little or no responsibility for anything themselves?

They seem trapped in victimhood and are impervious to the notion that they might have some responsibility for their own life experience. It's all your, his, her, their, or its fault. They may blame others when it's too embarrassing, inconvenient, or painful to look at their part in any given situation.

It's so much easier to project their pain onto someone else. Then they don't have to own any part of it themselves.

Usually, it begins with hurt feelings, sadness, or another strong primal emotion. Left untended, these feelings then morph into resentment, blame, and often anger.

Blame is the perfect self-awareness antidote. When we blame others, we relinquish our power to change.

What would a no-fault/no-blame life feel like?

CHALLENGING STUFF

...It turns out that you just weren't worth the faith I had in you.

JUDGMENT, BLAME, AND RESENTMENT

You spot it, you got it.

This aphorism is one of the hardest to understand and one of the hardest to accept. It points to our immense capacity for denial and self-deception.

If I see something in you that offends me, how do I notice it so clearly? Why does it jump out at me? Why does it bother me so much when it may have little or no effect on others?

"You spot it, you got it" suggests that anything I secretly dislike in myself will be greatly amplified when I notice it mirrored in you. When I see it, there's a shock of recognition, a familiarity. As familiar as it is, I find any part of it difficult to own. It's too embarrassing or painful to fathom. So, I project my distaste of it back on you, then blame you for it—for the very quality I abhor and deny in myself.

How do I so clearly notice how controlling you are? Well, because I can be controlling too. I feel safer that way. So instead of accepting our similarities and forgiving you for what I do too, I blame you for it. "Here, carry my controlling nature too." Then I won't have to admit it, take responsibility for it, or rectify it in myself.

It's a very insidious adaptation.

What grievances do you hold against yourself?

CHALLENGING STUFF

JUDGMENT, BLAME, AND RESENTMENT

> "What others think of me
> is none of my business."
> —Eleanor Roosevelt

Don't take anything personally.

Don Miguel Ruiz in his book, *The Four Agreements,* says the following in agreement two: "Don't take anything personally. Nothing others do is because of you. What others say and do is a projection of their own reality, their own dream. When you are immune to the opinions and actions of others, you won't be the victim of needless suffering."

I don't know about you, but I used to take everything personally. Pretty grandiose, right? I didn't understand that things might happen to me but weren't necessarily because of or about me.

There are so many forces in the world that are either random, accidental, or simply mysterious that have absolutely nothing to do with me. After all, I am not the center of the universe, only a small insignificant part, and temporary at that. To think otherwise causes much unnecessary distress.

What do you take personally that causes you distress?

CHALLENGING STUFF

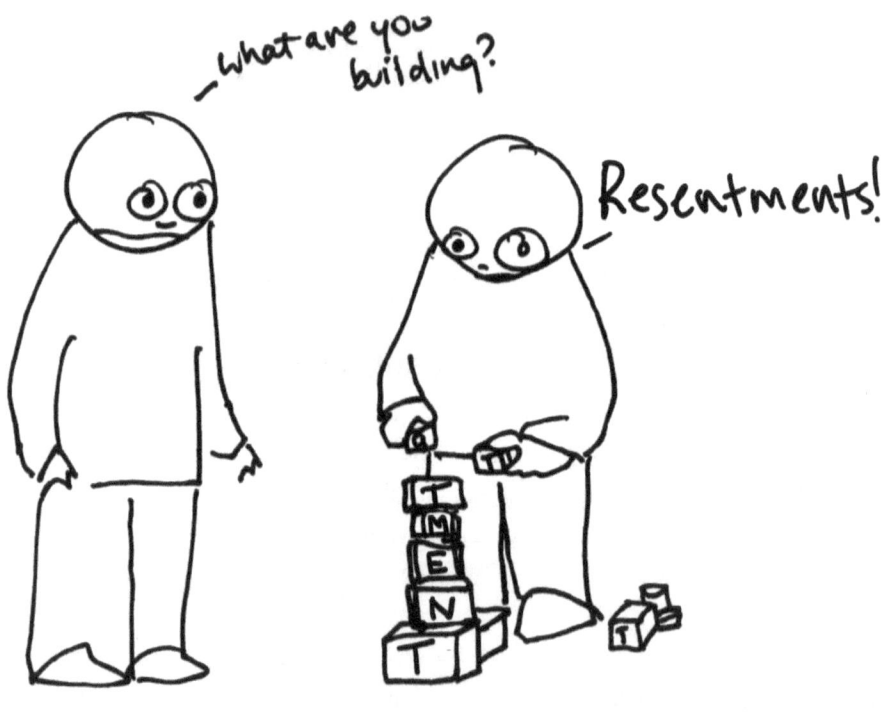

JUDGMENT, BLAME, AND RESENTMENT

"Expectations are resentments under construction."—Anne Lamott

As a kid, I wanted to be an FBI frogman. I loved *Sea Hunt*, with Lloyd Bridges. I lived in that fantasy for a while. But, as I matured, reality set in. I recognized that my family was not altogether normal and definitely wasn't happy. We were plagued by mental illness, alcoholism, epilepsy, OCD, suicide, and high blood pressure that cut through my dad's family like a thresher in a wheat field.

I had great expectations, especially on holidays, and none of them came true. They soured instead, morphing into resentments. I carried those burdens in my heart for years, even as my life evolved and prospered. Ultimately these resentments poisoned my inner being. Even in success, I found it hard to appreciate the small things. Gratitude, happiness, and peace of mind were ever elusive.

Six months before my father died, I was giving my stepmom a break and took care of him for a week. One Sunday, I was heating his oyster stew, his favorite winter Sunday lunch. While stirring, I looked over at him sitting in his bow tie and jacket at the kitchen table overlooking the quiet snow-covered landscape and I said, "I'm sorry I wasn't a better son to you." He turned and said, "I'm sorry I wasn't a better father to you."

In that fleeting moment, the resentments that I had carried for years melted away as if they had never existed, and I wondered why I'd held them for so long.

What resentments plague your ability to love?

CHALLENGING STUFF

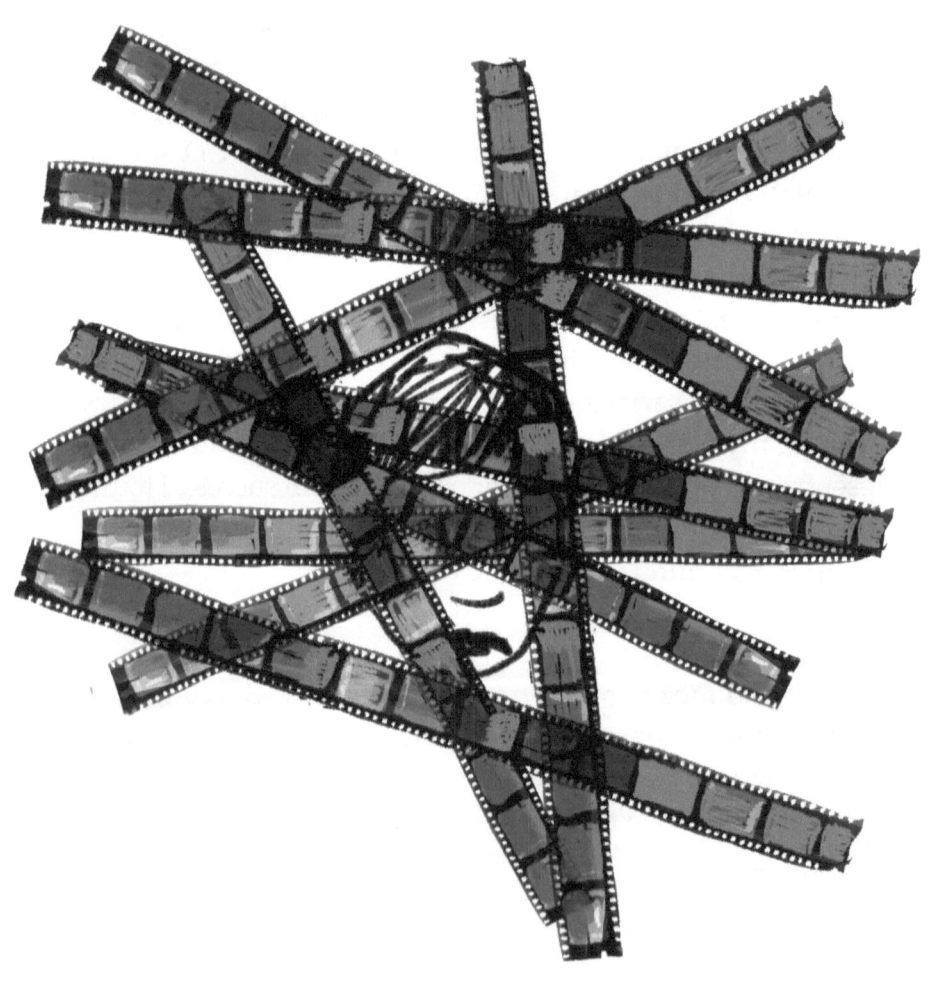

JUDGMENT, BLAME, AND RESENTMENT

Resentment is the darkroom where negatives are developed.

St. Augustine suggested that harboring a "resentment is like drinking poison and waiting for the other person to die."

Bitterness hurts us much more than those we resent. They are clueless. They couldn't care less. They go along their merry way, business as usual.

We, on the other hand, grind away in a brainstorm, allowing these resentments to live inside us rent-free. They disrupt our peace of mind, make us angry, and sicken our soul. Living in resentment is living in the dark space of anger. It's hard to see anything else.

"Remember, you belong to the thing with which you are linked in thought... When you hold resentment against another, you are bound to that person by a cosmic link, a real, though mental chain."—Emmet Fox, *The Sermon on the Mount*

Living in resentment is not in our best interest. We are worth far more than the resentments that plague our well-being and peace of mind. How does resentment disturb your life? How about letting some go?

What do you notice when you do?

CHALLENGING STUFF

JUDGMENT, BLAME, AND RESENTMENT

**If forced into the rain when young,
it's on them.
If you stay in the rain when grown,
it's on you.**

Now that you are an adult, how many childhood resentments do you harbor against your parents, relatives, friends, teachers, schools, etc.?

If there are some, then they've been festering for a very long time. They are deep-seated, embedded, and have become an integral part of your story. Most likely they hurt every time you think of them. Each one is like a little shock to your system—a jolt of anger, or sadness, or hurt, or pain. All of these little moments are woven into a story that becomes your mental movie, your narrative playing over and over again, saddening your soul.

"It is plain that a life which includes deep resentment leads only to futility and unhappiness... this business of resentment is infinitely grave."—Bill Wilson, *Alcoholics Anonymous*

Many things that happened in our childhoods were not our fault. But how we choose to live our adult lives *is* our responsibility. "We can't always choose the music life plays for us but we can choose how we dance to it."—Unknown

How would you like to rewrite your story?

CHALLENGING STUFF

JUDGMENT, BLAME, AND RESENTMENT

Put down the magnifying glass and pick up the mirror.

The primary tool of the self-righteous is the magnifying glass. The primary tool of the self-aware is self-reflection. Everything that happens around and to me is filtered through me so I can make sense of it—catalog, judge, accept, attack, defend. If these conditions are not to my liking, I may try to change them. This is often impossible, creating anger and frustration.

Thomas Merton suggests, "To consider persons and events and situations only in the light of their effect upon myself is to live on the doorstep of hell. . . For I cannot make the universe obey me."

We tend to look outside for the causes behind our problems, but usually the causes are closer to home. Shakespeare noted, "Things are neither good or bad but thinking makes it so." If I have a problem, the problem is me. The problem is in my thinking. Did I obsess? Did I blame or resent? Did I meddle? Did I try to fix it? Did I give unwanted advice? Did I procrastinate? Often, what I try to do as a result of my unmanageable thinking makes things worse.

Socrates suggests, "The unexamined life is not worth living." That might be a slight exaggeration but, in my experience, the examined life is more interesting, more peaceful, more fulfilling. Self-awareness invites me to realize myself and the world around me in heightened new ways and leaves others free to do the same.

What do you see when you look in the mirror?

Fear, Pain, and Worry

Don't trouble trouble 'til trouble troubles you

CHALLENGING STUFF

Much of my fear was based on false evidence appearing real.

FEAR, PAIN, AND WORRY

> "I've been absolutely terrified every moment of my life —and I've never let it keep me from doing a single thing I wanted to do."
> —Georgia O'Keeffe

When you are being chased by a bunch of velociraptors, it makes sense to be scared shitless and run like hell. Fear energizes our survival instinct and has served us well over millennia. When going to your car at night alone, it makes sense to be alert and practice situational awareness. It's prudent. In many instances, fear keeps us safe and alive.

But fear isn't always situational or time-sensitive. A rapacious predator, it can consume us over time. It can be irrational. It can be addictive, stunting our best intentions, our desires, and our dreams. Fear of failure, fear of the unknown, fear of others, or just plain free-floating fear with no specific focus or origin—the possibilities are endless.

What's the solution? Much like everything else in the thinking world, we are invited to pause and evaluate from a more rational perspective. Are our fears in proportion to our current circumstances? Are they overblown because they have been triggered by old events that no longer exist? Would it be helpful to face these fears and work through them instead of avoiding them?

What is it like to inhabit your own authority?

CHALLENGING STUFF

Then WHAM!!!!, out of nowhere, we are back in the tall grass...

FEAR, PAIN, AND WORRY

Back in the tall grass… again.

The world can be unrelentingly cruel. We have all experienced times of great strife and hardship. None of us are immune. How do we retain our balance and sanity in moments of crisis?

For days, maybe weeks, maybe months, maybe years, we're going along swimmingly. Then, *WHAM!*

Out of nowhere, we are back in the tall grass again, blinded, wondering how things went so wrong, so fast, hitting so hard.

We try not to take it personally, to step aside and view the situation from a distance, detaching from the intensity of the chaos and our own overwhelming emotions. This is not easy. It's hard but worthwhile. It offers a time out, a respite, an opportunity to gain composure and perspective we couldn't see in the tall grass.

In this new space, perhaps only seconds long, we call on all our tools: common sense, clear thinking, the counsel of others, and our understanding that, as the poet Hakim Sanai once wrote, "this too shall pass."

How do you find your way out of the tall grass?

CHALLENGING STUFF

FEAR, PAIN, AND WORRY

Worry is like peanuts.
You can't eat just one.

My worry seeker is always scraping the inside of my skull to find more stuff to worry about. That's his job. He takes it seriously. I tell myself, "If there is really something wrong, I don't have to go look for it. It will pop up again eventually." But my worry seeker is relentless and will have none of that!

If I were to gather up all of my worries over the years, they would fill a gigantic warehouse. Sadly, they wouldn't be worth a plug nickel.

What has that worry ever done for me? Did it help? No, not one bit. I often wonder how I could have spent so much time and energy doing something so utterly worthless and harmful.

Maybe worry creates an illusion of control. If I worry enough about this thing in the future, I might be able to find a solution before that future arrives. Or if I worry and bargain enough with the mistakes of the past, they will magically disappear, and I will be absolved. Worry becomes my penance for errors of the past and for future events already ruined.

Erma Bombeck suggests, "Worry is like a rocking chair: it gives you something to do but never gets you anywhere."

How can you worry less and enjoy more?

CHALLENGING STUFF

FEAR, PAIN, AND WORRY

Catastrophic "disasterbation"

Obsessive worry and fear can lead to catastrophic "disasterbation." Life is rife with numerous cognitive distortions. At times, we are irrational, confused, and even out of our minds. Fear and worry can infect us to such a degree that we become paralyzed, destabilized, and sure that all is lost.

"The sky is falling! The sky is falling!"

Sometimes, we just can't make sense of it all. We ruminate and obsess, regretting the past and worrying about the future. What a waste of time and energy.

Oddly enough, the future always shows up and usually far exceeds our negative expectations. It is often better than we could have imagined.

Sure, real fear can be a warning, a message to watch out and take the appropriate steps, but that's not what we are discussing here.

Leo Buscaglia reminds us, "Worry never robs tomorrow of its sorrow. It only saps today of its joy."

What tangible benefit have you ever gained from worry?

CHALLENGING STUFF

FEAR, PAIN, AND WORRY

> **"If we do not transform our pain, we will most assuredly transmit it."**
> **—Richard Rohr**

When I first heard these words spoken, they sent shockwaves through me. For the first time in my life, I understood how generational pain is inherited. How the pain in my family of origin had passed from generation to generation. I saw how the pain transmitted to me by my parents was now being transmitted by me to my wife and sons.

The biblical idea of "the sins of the father visited upon the sons" made more sense to me. And what is the sin? It is the lack of self-awareness—the sin is not interrupting the inheritance and not taking responsibility for my part in transmitting it. The sin is not fixing my broken parts but instead handing them down for another generation to carry.

Charles Eads said, "Hurt people hurt people." My job is to get well and get ready to break that cycle so that those who follow are free of those burdens. Heck, they will have plenty of their own.

What pain will you stop transmitting?

CHALLENGING STUFF

FEAR, PAIN, AND WORRY

Pain is inevitable, suffering optional.

Perspective is everything.

We all experience pain—some more than others, some so excruciating it's a wonder it can be survived. But the degree to which we suffer that pain is discretionary. This notion seems absurd when in the center of such extreme pain, but as the pain wanes we do have some say in the degrees to which we suffer it.

Do we let the pain define our future? Or, over time, can we learn to ameliorate it and let it go, morphing it into a story about our past that doesn't continue to trigger us emotionally?

President Lincoln, who suffered severe bouts of depression, once said, "People are about as happy as they make up their mind to be."

What suffering are you tolerating?

CHALLENGING STUFF

FEAR, PAIN, AND WORRY

"Get off the cross, honey. We need the wood."
—Dolly Parton

Self-pity is a subversive form of manipulation, enlisting others in support of our misery, of our self-inflicted victimhood. It has also been described as depressed narcissism, vanity's emotional amplifier.

In *The Little Red Book* (Hazelden Foundation), self-pity is described as "an extreme form of self-centeredness and is often outright rebellion against circumstances of our own making."

Self-pity is very different from sadness or grief, which are legitimate and eventually pass. This indulgently defeatist mentality is more of a way of life for some, consuming valuable internal resources that could be put to better use in the world.

If we stay locked in our pain, resentment, and hurt, nothing will change. If this is the only story we can tell, what of our future? It is forever lost to us and to those we love. We stay cemented in time and all the beauty in the world passes us by.

Since we are human and fallible, it stands to reason that some regrets are inevitable, a byproduct of not being aware enough early enough to make a difference. But we can't let that regret consume us.

Maya Angelou wrote, "I did then what I knew how to do. Now that I know better, I do better."

What part does self-pity play in your life?

CHALLENGING STUFF

"Anger is one letter short of danger."
—Eleanor Roosevelt

Anger is a secondary emotion, deriving its force and power from accumulated pain with no acceptable way to express itself. It is like the whistle on a teakettle, warning that if capped, the kettle might explode.

Anger is primitive—fight or flight. As a child, I had no way to express my sadness, hurt, or disappointment, so I got angry instead. I threw tantrums. The more they told me my anger was inappropriate, the angrier I got. Then, as time passed, instead of expressing it outwardly, I turned it inward against myself—holding resentments and self-loathing that threatened to tear me apart.

I later realized that it was necessary to understand these origins of my anger. Like deep roots, they reach way back and when activated by similar feelings in the present, trigger each other and explode with immense power, power expressed in anger that is not always proportional to the circumstance at hand, power that is hurtful and often scary to others.

These heightened emotional responses call on a higher degree of self-awareness, understanding and restraint. Pause and take inventory. Cool off. Then, instead of reacting, try to respond appropriately.

How is anger dangerous for you?

CHAPTER 6

Inevitable Stuff

We can try to tell time, but time always tells us.

I tell myself, "I want to do such and such by next month." Often, that deadline comes and goes, and the goal is not met. (I wonder why it's called a deadline. Talk about ratcheting up the consequences.) Why did I fail? Because I miscalculated, lost interest, or forgot.

I have no power over time; time powers itself with little regard to my insignificance. Time says, "I don't think so, Art. Better luck next time." Or, "Time to change your approach." Or, "You keep making the same mistake underestimating how much time it will take."

Often, we try to bargain with the past, but time doesn't go backwards. We try to pull time forward but that's delusional, of course. Even so, we try to speed up time to get to our better futures quicker. But we know that's a recipe for disaster

INEVITABLE STUFF

because we miss so much in between and ultimately get to our destination more slowly—"Are we there yet?"

Time itself is inevitable and no matter how much we try to control, manipulate or ignore it, it just moves on in spite of us. Don't do tomorrow's work today. Tomorrow will get here soon enough. You can do it then. Time takes its own sweet time.

Past, Present, and Future

"Today is the tomorrow you worried about yesterday."
—Dale Carnegie

INEVITABLE STUFF

The past is a black hole. Don't get too close, you may fall in.

PAST, PRESENT, AND FUTURE

"When your future arrives, will you blame your past?"
—Robert Half

"Yesterday is history. Tomorrow is a mystery. Today is a gift. That's why we call it the present."—Eleanor Roosevelt

One way to suffer is to argue with what was, what is, or what might be.

"Yesterday is a canceled check, tomorrow is a promissory note, today is the only cash you have—spend it wisely."—Kay Lyons

Bury your past or it will bury you.

You can't fix today with yesterday; you can't fix the present with the past.

When your emotions are disproportionate to the present circumstances, you're either regretting the past or anxious about the future.

"It isn't the burdens of today that drive men mad. It is the regrets over yesterday and the fear of tomorrow. Regret and fear are twin thieves who rob us of today."—Robert Hastings

The past is better forgotten. The future is better unknown. The present is the ultimate gift and is better lived moment to moment.

"It's okay to look back. Just don't stare."—Doris Roberts

"The best thing about the future is it comes one day at a time."—Abraham Lincoln

CHAPTER 7

Good Stuff

Okay, finally! We have been trudging around in some difficult stuff for a while. Now, let's turn to some better stuff: relationships, forgiveness, humility, and acceptance.

Aspirational as these topics might seem, don't be fooled. A whole lot of bad thinking is possible in these areas as well. In fact, it could be argued that thinking in this context can even be more insidious, more debilitating, and more hurtful because it lives in such stark contrast to the positive terrain it inhabits.

Relationship and Forgiveness

*"Without memory, there is no healing.
Without forgiveness, no future."*
—Desmond Tutu

GOOD STUFF

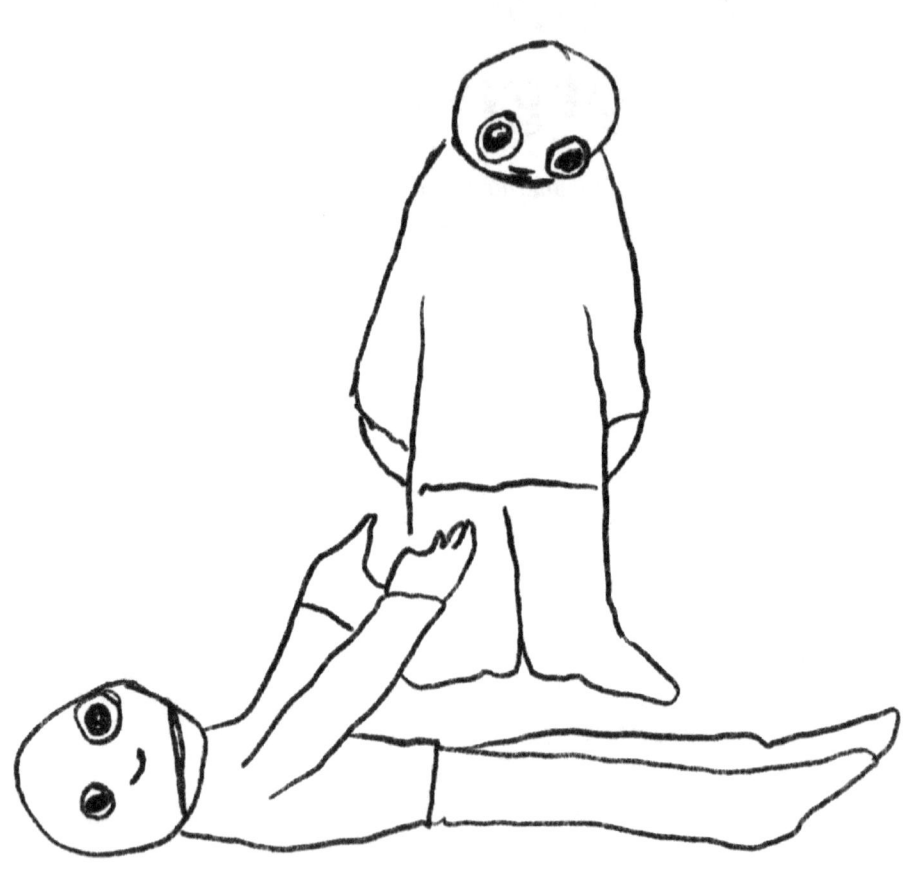

RELATIONSHIP AND FORGIVENESS

If you break some eggs, make an omelet.

Yeah, and don't cry over spilled milk either!

Life's recurring question is, "When you're knocked down, will you get up?"

This life is a test of our fierceness and our endurance. We have been and will get knocked down time and time again. Our only real choice is to get up again. The other choices pale in comparison.

- When you get a lemon, make lemonade.
- The glass is never half empty. It's always half full.
- If you fall off the horse, get back on.
- If you break some eggs, make an omelet.

I used to hate all these clichés. They pissed me off. "Can't you see that I'm hurt? Can't you see that I'm in pain? Can't you see how they cheated me? Can't you understand that I-I-I-Me-Me-Me?"

The hard truth is that nobody cares. Oh, they may care momentarily, but ultimately, *I* am responsible for my life's trajectory. *I* can either, "make it or break it."

When have you wanted to throw in the towel? Did you?

GOOD STUFF

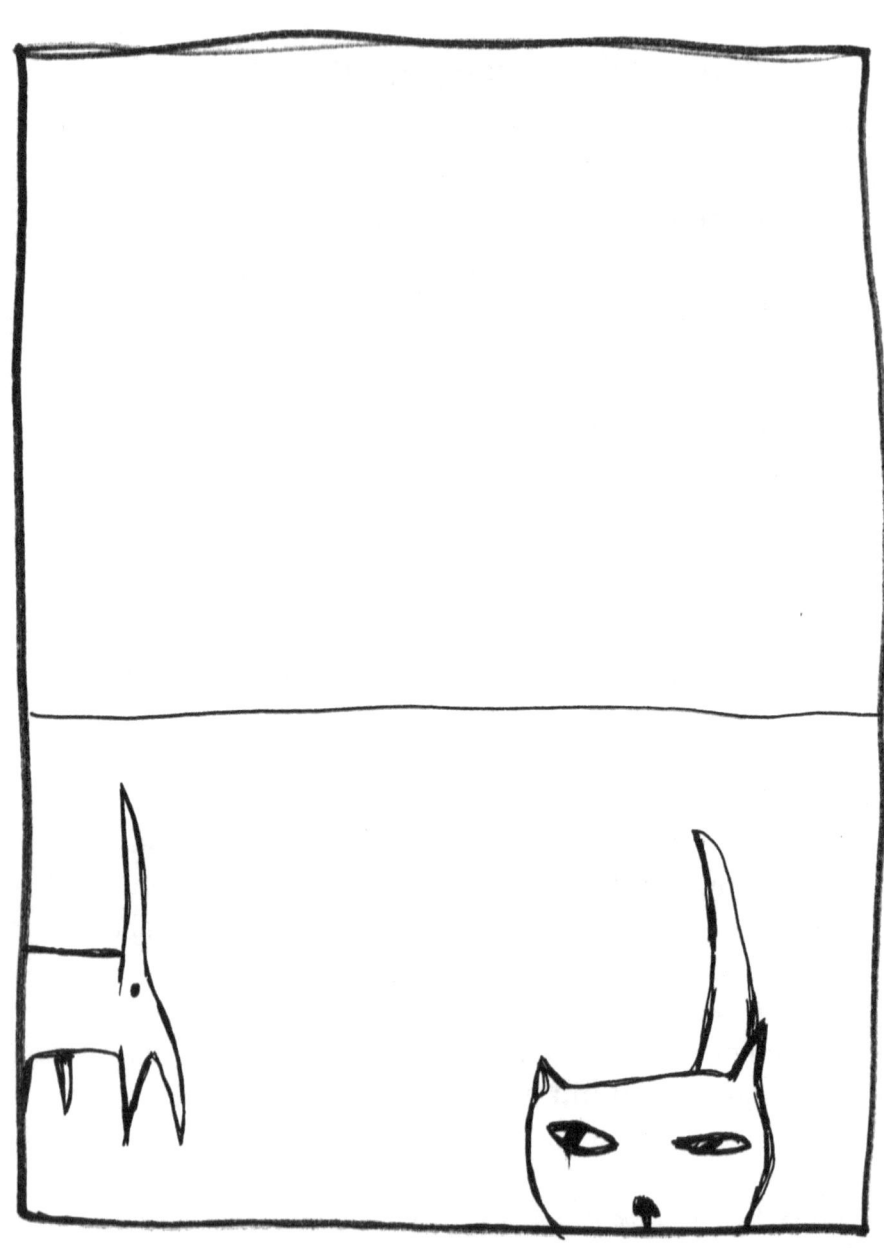

Better together apart.

"Better together apart" has been true for me, even with some family members and friends. Oil and water don't mix, and it can be kinder to all concerned to keep a safe distance.

I used to think it was my personal failure that I couldn't get along with some people. After all, we were grownups; we should be able to work it out. Now I realize that it's okay.

We aren't one-size-fits-all. Some people don't work for us. We don't work for some people. No harm, no foul. We aren't each other's kettle of fish. We don't have to feel guilty. We can accept our differences, appreciate our similarities, and allow the space necessary for all concerned to thrive in their own special way.

We should spend our time with those we love, with those who support and love us, especially with those who enhance the life we have chosen for ourselves.

What are you tolerating?

RELATIONSHIP AND FORGIVENESS

I'm going to take your temperature to see how I feel.

Growing up, my mood was often dictated by those around me. If they were unhappy, I was unhappy. If they were sad, it would make me sad. If they were okay, I was okay. My antennae were always up to gauge how the wind was blowing. I wasn't aware of this tendency for a long time. It was a survival technique developed early on. It served me well or so I thought. I considered my behavior as selfless, accommodating, and helpful.

But it wasn't. It was a form of cowardice. I was hiding. I was living through others for fear of living myself. As Louise L. Hay puts it, "How empty of me to be so full of you."

I kept twisting myself to conform to other people's needs. My needs didn't feel safe. It always seemed better to be a chameleon, detached from myself and attached to you. To not be abandoned, I abandoned myself.

Dennis Merritt Jones postulates, "Many of us live in denial of who we truly are because we fear losing someone or something—and there are times that if we don't rock the boat, too often the one we lose is ourselves… It feels good to be accepted, loved, and approved of by others, but often the membership fee to belong to that club is far too high of a price to pay."

Why stay in your own hula hoop?

GOOD STUFF

RELATIONSHIP AND FORGIVENESS

Putting your family first doesn't mean putting yourself last.

"I am only as happy as my least happy child." I believed this saying for many years. Sadly, it reeks of victimhood, self-pity, and martyrdom. This tendency to sacrifice for others is noble, no doubt, but is it always wise?

This sacrificial practice can be insidious in families, especially for parents. *The Parent Manual* teaches us to do everything we can for our children, to sacrifice for their well-being, to support them no matter what. Even take the bullet if necessary. Evolution and the next generation depend on it.

But what if they don't want what we have? What if they want what they want instead? What if they have their own ideas, dreams, and desires? (Of course they do.)

Some wise person once said, "The journey of parenthood is the constant process of letting go."

My children faced some difficult obstacles. I always wanted to try to fix, alleviate, manage, protect, and solve. But the more I tried, the more my life became unmanageable. At a certain point, I realized I was powerless over their lives and futures.

I was forced to let go and turn them over to "life's longing for itself."—Kahlil Gibran, "On Children"

How can you let go and take better care of yourself?

GOOD STUFF

RELATIONSHIP AND FORGIVENESS

My loved ones know how to push my buttons. They installed them.

My mom, bless her heart, in addition to all of her good qualities, had a certain proclivity for judgment. The minute I walked into the room, I could sense an opinion brewing that I always interpreted as a judgment. And many times it was.

"Is that really what you're going to wear?" she would ask, or, "I see you've done something with your hair." On seeing me sign a check, she once said, "Well, that's not much of a signature!"

I loved my mom, but honestly, sometimes she could really piss me off. I swore I would never be like her. She no doubt inherited this skill from her mother, Bertha, who was a judgment rock star, and she no doubt picked it up from her parents. And so it goes. And guess what? I'm judgmental too! What a surprise.

I have come to believe that judgment is a salve for self-loathing. It's a deflection or misdirection from one's own discomfort or insecurity. Instead of judging others, practice self-management and self-care. It's not selfish, it's self-aware and nutritious.

How does judgment impede you?

GOOD STUFF

RELATIONSHIP AND FORGIVENESS

I'm not forgiving you for you.
I'm forgiving you for me.

Sometimes some things can't be forgiven. They are just too hurtful, painful, or destructive. They seem unforgivable. They live inside … festering. They are like splinters under fingernails, that can't be extracted. They are always bothersome, looping around in our memory, becoming long-held remnants that poison our story.

In his book, *Breathing Under Water,* Richard Rohr suggests, "Forgiveness is to let go of our hope for a different or better past."

There are many things in my past I have forgiven because I'm tired of lugging them around. They are heavy, loathsome, and ruinous. I may not like it but I must forgive for my own sanity and peace of mind. If I want to move forward, I must forgive the fallibility of others.

What about my own fallibility? As I become more aware of the worlds around me, I also become more aware of the worlds within me. I can't escape, deny, or repress my transgressions anymore. It's too painful, weighing heavily on my heart. Life calls me to a higher standard, to be aware of my actions and when in error, make amends ASAP!

What can't you forgive?

GOOD STUFF

Leave your past behind
or
be dragged by it.

Our life journey is dependent on our ability to release each other and ourselves from the burdens of the past that seem to drag us, distorting our present and poisoning our future.

Dwelling on the past can be toxic and at times make living torturous. Thoughts invade time after time, swirling and driving us mad in the process. But like stray cats, they only return if we feed them. "They have no life of their own other than what we give them."—Emmet Fox

We are human—imperfect. We all make mistakes, and we all hurt those we love. Their proximity reverberates in the imperfection of our humanness. It's inevitable. In life's search for its better self, it implores us to admit our wrongs, apologize, and make amends. It implores us to move past our past to relish the present and build better futures.

What baggage can you leave behind?

Humility and Acceptance

We are imperfect but still limited editions.

GOOD STUFF

HUMILITY AND ACCEPTANCE

> "There is a ghost in every house,
> and if you make peace with him,
> he will stay quiet."
> —Graham Greene,
> *The Quiet American*

Sometimes it feels like there are many ghosts in my house (and my brain). They run around constantly infusing me with regret, guilt, and self-doubt.

They may be the ghosts of people I've known, of things unsaid, promises broken, apologies ignored, mistakes made, or people I've hurt. Or they may just be random electrical impulses that download on my mental hard drive—haunting me, making me uncomfortable, restless, and discontented.

I think these ghosts are fragments of my shadow self, stuck in my unconscious. They yearn for reconciliation. They keep popping out to remind me, to nudge me, to implore me to do whatever is necessary to lay them to rest. I must learn to make peace with them or they will continue to make war with me.

Where could you make things right?

GOOD STUFF

HUMILITY AND ACCEPTANCE

Acceptance doesn't require our approval.

There are many things that have happened in our lives that we don't approve of, some of which were outside of our control. But there are also things we have done ourselves that we don't approve of. We have made mistakes, we have regrets, we have not always lived up to the person we wanted to be. Sometimes we have fallen short.

Many of these things have plagued our thought life for years. We have resisted them, tried to repress them, or forget them altogether.

They are always there, hidden in the shadows. We don't have to condone or approve of anything we have done, or others have done to us. But we do have to accept the truth of these events and transgressions. If we don't, there will always be a cognitive dissonance impossible to reconcile.

What are you still hiding?

GOOD STUFF

HUMILITY AND ACCEPTANCE

If I have a problem, the problem is me. I am the jailer, the jailed, and the key.

This aphorism is a keystone to understanding and is one of the most difficult to accept. At first, it seems so paradoxical and impossible: "NO! All my problems come from my boss, my family, my computer, my car, my girlfriend," and on, and on. It's the outside world that creates the inside disturbances I suffer.

Sometimes, my computer goes all wacky. When it does, I panic: "I've lost data, I have a virus, the Russians co-opted my hard drive, the world is ending!" I freak out. Self-loathing takes over. "You're terrible at this! What did you do now? Why did you push that key? You're a frigging idiot!" Then I call my computer guy, Jerry, tell him what's happened, and he says, "Hit control something or other," and magically it's all fixed. For me, it was a monumental crisis of historic proportions. For Jerry, it was a simple fix; same event, two vastly different reactions.

I am a product of my own thinking, my own perceptions and my own feelings. It's how I see things that define my ease or dis-ease. The world is mercurial, but I don't have to be. I can recalibrate. Turns out things don't have to be okay for me to be okay.

"For there is nothing either good or bad, but thinking makes it so." —William Shakespeare, *Hamlet*

How do you retain your serenity?

GOOD STUFF

HUMILITY AND ACCEPTANCE

"Wherever you go, there you are."
—Jon Kabat-Zinn

In my twenties, after completing my military service, I had a choice to work in New York City (not far from my hometown) or to head west. It was an easy choice. I packed up my black VW Hatchback and hit the road heading to Denver, then San Francisco, and finally to Los Angeles.

I convinced myself that I was driving west for work. And that was true, but the hidden emotional drive was to escape my family of origin.

I was chasing a new future, but I was still the main character, still wrapped in the pain and dysfunction I so desperately wanted to leave behind. So, I pulled a "geographic." I moved three thousand miles away for a clean start while painstakingly pulling my same old emotional baggage in tow.

I thought I could outrun my past, but I could never outrun myself. Trust me, I tried.

What are you running from?

GOOD STUFF

HUMILITY AND ACCEPTANCE

"Mama said there'd be days like this."
—The Shirelles

Some days just plain suck!

I wake up on the wrong side of my head and I can't see the forest for the trees. I try to alter my thinking, but old gloom-and-doom is doing pushups in the corner, and I can't shake the feeling that hangs in the air. Maybe I ate something that didn't agree with me, maybe I made a mistake that I can't forgive, maybe some days just suck and there's no rhyme or reason to it.

When I feel this way, I ask the question, "What's really going on here? How can I get to the bottom of it and redirect this lousy feeling?" If I can get to the bottom of it, all the better. There is understanding there. But often the reasons are elusive. So, I decide to act as if all is well. I remind myself to take it one day at a time, that I can sleep tonight and wake tomorrow renewed.

Resetting the day is the skill of interruption, by distracting the bad with something better, reaching out to others, being of service, journaling, exercising, meditating or anything that gets me going again.

Sometimes, I just have to make the radical decision to get out of my own way.

How do you turn around a bad day?

GOOD STUFF

HUMILITY AND ACCEPTANCE

"Your best teacher is your last mistake."
—Ralph Nader

I love victories! They are thrilling, exhilarating, and welcoming.

My mistakes, on the other hand, are embarrassing, painful, and sometimes costly. They make me question myself. I begin to doubt my competency, my instincts.

Let's face it: Sometimes, the cheese slips off the cracker, we lose our keys, get a parking ticket, or worse, sometimes much worse. Mistakes are made. Often, it's a result of not paying enough attention to what's right in front of me. I am operating on autopilot or cruise control. I'm not sufficiently aware in the moment.

Both success and failure come with learning and understanding, but it is my mistakes that reverberate most. They stay with me longer, requiring real work and self-examination. It is in the core of my mistakes that I am truly vulnerable and powerless. They are hard to admit or face or rectify due to my own defensiveness or denial. But they are an integral part of the journey, of stretching, growing, risking, and moving into the unknown. In unwinding them, I learn the most about myself.

What did your most recent mistake teach you?

GOOD STUFF

HUMILITY AND ACCEPTANCE

Sometimes I crave the inconsequential.

Do you get tired of everything mattering so much?

Mark Manson suggests the following in his book, *The Subtle Art of Not Giving a F*ck:* "Giving too many fucks is bad for your mental health. It causes you to become overly attached to the superficial and fake, to dedicate your life to chasing a mirage of happiness and satisfaction. The key to life is not giving a fuck about more; it's giving a fuck about less, giving a fuck about only what is true and immediate and important."

Let's face it: Life is jam-packed and caring about everything is exhausting. Everything seems urgent and important. Pick your battles and make choices based on your own core values. Be selective and don't sweat the small stuff. After all, there are so many hours in the day, and it's important to spend some of them wasting time!

Alternatively, as Steven Covey suggests, seek true recreation. Consider the structure of this word for a moment: re-creation. By taking time to stop, rest, take stock, and do things that are pleasurable, by interrupting the urgent day-to-day challenges and the chaos of the hamster wheel, we actually "re-create" our mental, physical, and spiritual states and, in so doing, return refreshed and renewed.

Do you feel guilty when you take time for yourself?

GOOD STUFF

HUMILITY AND ACCEPTANCE

> **"Completion comes not from adding another piece to ourselves but from surrendering our ideas of perfection."**
> —Mark Epstein

I used to think I was like Humpty Dumpty, all busted up, that I was incomplete, that the hole in my heart had to be filled, that I wasn't good enough, never enough. How could I possibly be satisfied with that?! Hell no! It was time to get a-fixin'!

So, I embarked on a journey of uncover, discover, and discard. I did lots of therapy, coaching, repairs, and piecing myself back together again. These, and other interventions, were all very helpful, but I still felt something was missing.

"Life is a journey, a path, a series of stages or steps or levels of development. The ego must be formed before it can be dismantled; the self must be consolidated before it can be transcended."—Mark Epstein, *Going to Pieces Without Falling Apart.*

Am I a better version today of who I was yesterday? Am I reconstituted? Am I different or am I still the same person experiencing life differently? I think the latter. Today, I live in new internal terrain, less focused on beefing myself up and more focused on letting myself go.

Is the lack you feel true or imagined?

GOOD STUFF

HUMILITY AND ACCEPTANCE

Happiness is appreciating what you have, not getting what you want.

Oh my gosh! This one is tricky—another of life's many paradoxes.

This aphorism seems to imply that we should stop striving to want better, get better, or be better. It suggests that we should just suck it up and not want anything other than what we have.

Conversely, if we are in a constant state of wanting, it's almost impossible to be satisfied with what we have. The constant state of wanting perpetually devalues what we already have. It devalues our efforts, our accomplishments, and our successes.

What if we don't focus on how far we have to go but instead appreciate how far we've come? Grow and develop, sure, but not at the expense of missing the moment. The moment is all we really have. It's where we are most alive. Everything else is a figment of our imagination. The past, present, and future are not irreconcilable if we are immersed in the vitality and appreciation of this exact sliver of time we inhabit.

The grass may not be greener on the other side. First, grow where you're planted.

Where are you right this second?

GOOD STUFF

HUMILITY AND ACCEPTANCE

Life on life's terms

What does "life on life's terms" mean anyway? I used to think that my life was on my own terms. Right? After all, I'm reasonably competent, reasonably educated, and I have free will, don't I? I get to choose.

Of course, as the years passed, many things happened that I did not choose, some good and some bad. I saw that life is capable of forging ahead without my advice, permission, or approval.

Now, I ride along and even participate at times, but I am not the arbiter of outcomes. I cannot outline my future no matter how much I try.

If you want to hear God laugh, tell Him your plans.

How can you accept life as it comes?

GOOD STUFF

HUMILITY AND ACCEPTANCE

The best I will ever be is human.

This is without a doubt my favorite aphorism. I reflect on it often.

It is so gentle, generous, and liberating, speaking eloquently to our frailty and incompleteness. It recognizes and accepts our strengths, struggles, and those parts of us that are broken both known and unknown. It forgives us for being less than perfect and acknowledges that we embody all that is human—both the good and the not so good.

It's also hopeful, inviting us to draw forth the best in ourselves and seek the best in others. We are often inundated by our defects and shortcomings. Certainly, relatives and friends have keen insight into those matters but what about our good qualities and assets?

Can you accept compliments for those qualities?

CHAPTER 8

Sweet Stuff

If there was ever a time for celebration, it's now. You're almost done reading this book! I hope you have enjoyed reading as much as I have writing.

We have all been through so much over the past few years. The world has been and continues to be a bit nuts. In the face of all this upheaval, often while quarantining, we have had an opportunity to delve into our own being—an opportunity to self-reflect in service to better thinking and higher consciousness.

What has become obvious, as I have spent this time alone, is the necessity of learning how to manage my own thoughts, especially the negative thoughts that are so detrimental to my productivity and enjoyment in life. In doing so, I'm gifted again and again with less anxiety, a fuller spirit, and enormous gratitude.

SWEET STUFF

My spirit is dependent on the thoughts that precede it. As Emmet Fox consistently suggests, "When the spirit is right, the details will take care of themselves."

Spirit and Awareness

We are spirit having a human experience

SWEET STUFF

SPIRIT AND AWARENESS

> "It is better to light a single candle than to curse the darkness."
> —Eleanor Roosevelt

I vividly remember the day I moved into my apartment after twenty-eight years of marriage. We had separated. By mutual agreement, we knew it was time to try something new.

Nonetheless, there was sadness and regret. The loneliness and heartache of not being a better husband and not living with my children in the same house under the same roof were crushing me.

So, I kept busy arranging the few items I had moved: a few chairs, tables, an air mattress, some books, and a few lamps—one of which was a jug lamp that I inherited from my grandmother.

As the day descended into darkness, so did my mood. The feelings of sadness I had been ignoring all day swept over me. I felt completely alone. The only thing I could think to do was find the perfect place for that jug lamp and turn it on. And I did. The result was palpable. Something turned back on in me, too.

Where do you find your light?

SWEET STUFF

SPIRIT AND AWARENESS

> **"The darker the night, the brighter the stars."**
> —Apollon Maykov

If I were to ask, "What are the qualities of love?" you might answer, "affection, caring, kindness, embrace, intimacy," and many others. Sadly, at certain times in life, the most prevalent quality of love is *grief*.

I used to think of love and grief as opposites, but they're not. Love and hate are opposites. Grief and joy are opposites. Love and grief are inextricably linked.

They were born together, sharing much of the same DNA. They don't look alike but walk the path hand in hand as fraternal twins.

As Megan Devine put it in her book, *It's OK That You're Not OK:* "Grief is visceral, not reasonable; the howling at the center of grief is raw and real. It is love in its most wild form. There is nothing wrong with grief. It's a natural extension of love. It's a healthy and sane response to loss. That grief feels bad doesn't make it bad; that you feel crazy doesn't make you crazy. Grief is part of love. Love for life, love for self, love for others. What you are living, painful as it is, is love. And love is really hard. Excruciating at times."

What is good grief?

SWEET STUFF

SPIRIT AND AWARENESS

My emotional wellness is directly correlated to my spiritual condition.

As a younger man, I paid some attention to my physical self, my thought self, and my emotional self (the latter falling into two categories: good and bad emotions). Wanting and doing and having defined my being. The notion of spirituality completely escaped me. I couldn't have even discussed it. I had no idea what the word meant. Spirit was a church thing. I rarely went.

At the time, I didn't realize that my spirit was already alive in me, peeking out from time to time connecting me to something even greater than my own self-interest; the sun streaming through the clouds after a rain shower, children's laughter, a bed of roses. These and other moments were fleeting hints at the beauty life could be if I could only allow it.

As the years pass now, I have less to prove or defend. My emotional life is calmer as I shift my emphasis from doing to being. I was given something early in life that is now revealing itself, the very gift of my life's spirit that already holds intrinsic value far beyond my awareness of it.

How do you nurture your spirit?

SWEET STUFF

SPIRIT AND AWARENESS

If you're always over there then you're never really over here.

"Hello? Dad! Distracted or what? Snap out of it and join the party."

Thousands of times every day I find my mind over there when my body is over here. Sometimes, my body even goes over there too, so none of me is over here. Hello! What just happened? Was I transported or shape shifted? I left the moment here with you and found myself somewhere else in the fog.

"Beam me up, Scotty."

I've seen that mental shift triggered in others, too. My dad was a music teacher, an epileptic, an alcoholic, and very self-involved. When I would visit him on the weekends he would hug me—you know, one of those uncomfortable man hugs where you're afraid to actually touch—and then he would disappear into his own world. He was rarely, if ever, here with me, but instead over there in his own protective bubble.

Our preoccupation with self often leaves those in our midst abandoned.

What is it like for you to stay here?

SWEET STUFF

SPIRIT AND AWARENESS

Don't spend your day un-meditated.

What is meditation anyway? For me, it goes something like this: meditation is the decision to stop thinking about thought—having a thought but choosing not to engage with it.

Here's an analogy used by my teacher. Imagine you're sitting by the side of the road watching the cars go by. And let's say that each car is a bunch of "thought worms." There are *lots* of cars, hundreds per hour. You decide to stop watching the cars and jump right into the middle of the street to direct traffic. Cars speeding by, you find yourself zigzagging to avoid being hit. Afraid for your life, you desperately want to leap to safety.

Meditation is the choice to stay out of traffic, to sit quietly by the side of the road, and to let the cars pass by, each car a group of thoughts "arising, enduring, and passing away."
—James Finley, *The Contemplative Heart*.

Thought is inevitable. Engaging with thought is optional. When meditating, we become the observer of thought instead of the thinker of thought.

How does meditation enhance your experience?

SWEET STUFF

SPIRIT AND AWARENESS

"The breath breathes itself."
—Jack Kornfield

So much of what we do and who we are is unconscious. We take it for granted because it's so automatic.

We are powerless over it. Just decide to stop breathing and see how far you get. Try not eating, or sleeping, or loving, or the thousands of other things that we take for granted every day without a second thought. We are driven by forces both mysterious and divine.

I used to think that I was doing the breathing, but it's not true. My breath is a gift that is given to me. It breathes itself. I had no control when it started and will have no control when it ends. In each moment, I am riding the crest of life's breath. If I can sit with it and stay tuned, I can feel every moment of breath as the spirit of the universe breathes through me.

When I close my eyes and breathe, I come home. Do you?

Understanding and Gratitude

*"The first to apologize is the bravest.
The first to forgive the strongest.
The first to forget the happiest."*
—*Anonymous*

SWEET STUFF

UNDERSTANDING AND GRATITUDE

"Never ruin an apology with an excuse." —Benjamin Franklin

Have you ever noticed how sour an apology can be when followed by an excuse? Excuses and justifications fall on deaf ears because, well, they suck and no one wants to hear them. "I'm sorry, I don't have my homework. My cat ate it." "I apologize for forgetting your birthday. I've been so busy!" "I really didn't mean to hit you that hard, but you make me so mad."

When you follow an apology with an excuse, you negate the very apology you were trying to make in the first place. You probably thought you should make the apology but secretly didn't want to. So, you subtly shifted the locus of blame to feel less at fault yourself; to justify your actions that adversely affect others.

An apology followed by an excuse is actually not an apology at all. It's an insidious manipulation leaving others confused, unseen, and devalued.

"We ought to relentlessly ignore excuses, especially those we are told by ourselves."—Mokokoma Mokhonoana

How do you feel when people make excuses to you?

SWEET STUFF

UNDERSTANDING AND GRATITUDE

The same fire that melts the butter hardens the egg.

What doesn't kill you makes you stronger.

I don't know what trials and tribulations you have faced in your life, no doubt many. In my family tree we have premature death, divorce, suicide, addiction, job loss, broken friendships, betrayal, ill health, and the beat goes on. These events, far from unique, are visited upon all of us to one degree or another. We can't escape them. They are part of life's glorious imperfections.

When one of these events happens to me or someone I love, I am crushed, broken, and despondent. Ultimately, I am faced with a choice: will I let it destroy me or will I face the fire and rise above it?

My answer sometimes comes quickly, sometimes slowly, but is always, "I want to survive, to survive for myself and for those I love."

Life is relentless. It yearns for itself.

What do you yearn for today?

SWEET STUFF

UNDERSTANDING AND GRATITUDE

Don't go to a hardware store looking for milk.

Why do we often look for the stuff we need in all the wrong places? Maybe because we don't know what we need or even want. Maybe because life's direction manual is so confusing. It's impossible to outline the future. It's a bit of a guessing game.

People move to Los Angeles seeking fame and fortune when what they really want is love. The daughter of a lawyer becomes a lawyer, but she really wants to be a sculptor. We go to outer space seeking new planets when we don't even take care of our own. We drink or take drugs to feel better, but eventually feel worse.

The question is, how can you narrow the odds? Start by clarifying your values and core drivers. Drill down to understand what makes you a happy puppy. Then make choices in the world that correlate with those intrinsic values. These choices offer a higher probability of finding a fulfilling path.

But remember: "The path to fulfillment can be difficult, unfamiliar, and scary . . . Choosing to live our lives based on our values is not what society has taught us to do. It is not the easy, well-trodden way. Most of us settle for what we can have. We make choices based on what others want, what would be easiest, what would cause the least discomfort . . . We give up. It's no easy task to get on the track for fulfillment . . . In fact, we say choosing a fulfilling life is a radical act."—*Co-Active Coaching* by Laura Whitworth, Henry Kimsey-House, and Phil Sandahl.

What holds you back?

SWEET STUFF

UNDERSTANDING AND GRATITUDE

There's a place for everything and everything in its place.

This was my grandmother Bertha's favorite saying. She was a stickler for order and very old school. My mother was the same and guess what? I caught the gene too.

I've always liked order. I like the precision of it, the artistry and symmetry. Order has always made sense. Much like logic, structure, having a plan, being organized—all of these things appeal to me.

But why? Why are these traits so fundamentally important to me? I realized that they make me feel safe. They help me cope with the unknown, the unfathomable, with death itself. They help me cope with the disorder in the world, of life, and of my own thinking.

I like to think of myself as rational, in control, ordered. I work at it, and yet experience has taught me that when faced with circumstances above my pay grade, I'm as likely as the next guy to wig out. And I have.

Maybe the only real order is the natural order. Lao Tzu states, "The world is ruled by letting things take their course."

What's disordered in your life right now?

SWEET STUFF

UNDERSTANDING AND GRATITUDE

> *"No matter how lost you feel,
> life always reminds you who you are."*
> —La Veneno, *Veneno*

Life is indefatigable, constantly challenging us to rediscover who we are. It has a magical propensity for self-correction, recalibration, and reclamation. When we feel lost, life invites us to find our way. When sad, life brings laughter. When sick, we crave a return to health. When alone, we seek fellowship and love.

For years, I was unknown to myself. I just went with the program, followed the rules, and put one foot in front of the other. My socialization was complete. My false self prevailed, leaving me terrified to face my fears, my resentments, and my true identity.

It always seemed like I was bouncing up and down on a teeter-totter between what is expected and what is true for me. The fact is that my true self, my conscious spiritual self, was always there, stuck under the rubble.

Ultimately, life always reminds us who we are, seeking equilibrium, openness, honesty, and the willingness to share our true selves with ourselves and others.

Where are you holding back?

SWEET STUFF

UNDERSTANDING AND GRATITUDE

"Some don't cop to the cheese, no matter how many holes are in it."
—Anonymous

"There is no home for the soul in which there dwells the shadow of an untruth."—George Meredith.

Why do we lie and keep secrets? I think it's so we can do what we want even when we fear others might disapprove. Sometimes our will is stronger than the potential consequences.

We delude ourselves into thinking that secrets and lies will keep the peace when we are not aligned with each other. We tell ourselves, "What they don't know won't hurt them."

There's a well-known adage from Alcoholics Anonymous: "We're only as sick as our secrets." Secrets are not the safe harbor they are purported to be—quite the opposite. They are acts of defiance against our own integrity, defensive, and isolating, imprisoning us in the bondage of falsehood.

When dealing with others' secrets and lies, we feel insecure, confused, even angry and resentful. We sense the withholding, the drifting apart, the loss of trust.

"Lies have short legs."—German Proverb

What secrets pain you?

SWEET STUFF

UNDERSTANDING AND GRATITUDE

Hug a cactus once in a while.

Facing the lies we tell ourselves is a high form of humility. Sometimes, it's important to impersonate an evolved human being and actually tell the truth. But, as we all know, the truth is often hard to admit to oneself, let alone say out loud to others.

Telling the truth can feel prickly, like hugging a cactus. As a kid, I didn't choose the honesty option voluntarily. I much preferred keeping my cards close to the vest. When we built that fort in the woods, I didn't cop to stealing the materials from that construction site. It wasn't me who enjoyed scaring my sister to death! Look at me—I'm an angel. My response whenever accused was always, "Who, me?"

I was always defending, hiding, or trying to stay under the radar. If I shared the truth of my unhappiness and rage, I would surely be abandoned. So, my solution was to be an enigma, hard to read, presenting well on the outside but closed on the inside.

Luckily, I have since learned that the truth can in fact set me free. It's an acquired attribute, developed as I gained awareness of my own self-worth and, once realized, too painful to ignore.

What truth are you resisting?

SWEET STUFF

UNDERSTANDING AND GRATITUDE

Life works because we aren't all batshit crazy at the same time.

We are social beings. Our individual instabilities are often recalibrated through our connection with one other. When we are sad, or angry, or a little crazy we can reach out to our loved ones for support, solace, and advice. "A problem shared is a problem halved."—English Proverb

I am always reminded of this when I am going through one difficulty or another. My first instinct is to hide and figure it out myself. I may be too embarrassed or upset to talk with someone else, or I'm too damn angry and I don't want to admit it. The problem is, it's hard to solve a problem with a mind consumed by the problem.

Sometimes, just having someone listen is enough to settle our troubled minds and help us find new perspectives and strategize new solutions. As Helen Keller said, "Alone we can do so little; together we can do so much."

Most of us thrive in the middle of the herd. The closeness of life calms us, a constant reminder that we are part of life as it abounds—not separate from it.

Renuka Pitre suggests, "Sometimes, asking for help means you are helping yourself."

Why won't men ask for directions?

SWEET STUFF

UNDERSTANDING AND GRATITUDE

I'm already the person I've been searching for.

What if finding ourselves was less about searching, and more about being; less about wanting more, and more about wanting less, being satisfied with who and what we already are instead of wishing we were someone else?

Once again, grow where you're planted. If you want to move at a later date, that's fine. But take advantage of where you are to the fullest extent possible.

Wherever you go, there you are. Wherever we go in the world, we take our intelligence, spirit, and love along with our baggage.

We can try to run away from ourselves, but that usually doesn't end well. So, take advantage of what every situation, person, place, or thing has to offer you. There are great lessons to be learned everywhere and "every when."

As Oscar Wilde recommended, "Be yourself; everyone else is already taken."

What part of you yearns for expression?

SWEET STUFF

UNDERSTANDING AND GRATITUDE

> **"Just cause you got the monkey off your back doesn't mean the circus has left town."**
> —George Carlin

I am reminded daily that I am a work in progress; that progress not perfection is how it works. After all, the best I will ever be is human. And to be human is to be flawed. No matter how much I try, I am still flawed—sometimes in ways that are known and others that are more hidden.

As we endeavor to access our true selves through conscious awareness, we all still struggle with human tendencies to regress into default feelings, behaviors, habits, cognitive distortions, denial, blame, and self-will run riot. This *is* the circus and it's okay. It represents the breadth of our wondrously complex humanness.

This aphorism invites us to be a witness to our living self, to take personal inventory and responsibility if warranted. It challenges us to be vigilant and pay close attention to our lesser instincts and impulses so that our actions correlate more fully with who we want to be. This allows us to be free of some of the burdens we carry, to awaken and walk upright in the clear light of day.

What are you tolerating?

SWEET STUFF

UNDERSTANDING AND GRATITUDE

Gratitude is a little thing that makes a big difference.

Doris Day was known to say, "Gratitude is riches; complaint is poverty." It's hard to be angry, resentful, or fearful when full of gratitude. It is an amazing superpower. Thankfulness fills the space that is wanting. It's hard to feel bad when expressing gratitude.

A few years ago, I was invited to join a gratitude text list with some friends and we're still going strong. Every day I receive one or two lists and often contribute one of my own. Writing the list elevates my spirit, reminding me of all that I have, of how fortunate I am. When I'm in the dumps or things aren't going my way, it is especially important to pause, remember what I do have, and write the list. It never fails to turn me around.

In a culture of "never enough," driven by the dissatisfaction of wanting more, newer, bigger, and better, gratitude is seemingly out of place—an antiquated notion, an anachronism—but it's not. Life is grand when my gratitude outpaces my expectations.

"Be grateful for today; tomorrow is never promised."
—Anonymous

Write a list of ten things you're grateful for.
How do you feel now?

SWEET STUFF

UNDERSTANDING AND GRATITUDE

> "When people are laughing,
> they're generally not killing each other."
> —Alan Alda

This one doesn't need much explanation. It's obvious, isn't it? Laughter is one of the great and universal elixirs. Laughter is robust. It fills the sad and painful spaces.

I often think about my seventh-grade homeroom teacher, Mr. Ackley. He had a gift for drawing out the sad kids. He would look me in the eye and say, "I bet you can't *NOT* laugh in the next ten seconds."

We would all take the bet of course, knowing we would lose. He was a master of funny faces. They were hysterical. So, we gathered around on the playground or in the hallway and counted down. He would pucker his lips and pretend to be a flounder flopping on the dock, and in seconds, we were all laughing with joy.

It felt like he knew our sadness personally, that he carried it himself, felt its darkness, and in that moment of laughter and knowing, we didn't feel so alone anymore.

Mr. Ackley drove a red MG convertible. He named it Edith. We thought that was funny, too.

Have you laughed today? Why not?

SWEET STUFF

UNDERSTANDING AND GRATITUDE

"Never let the fear of striking out keep you from playing the game." —Babe Ruth

Satchel Paige, the great Hall of Fame baseball pitcher, is credited with saying, "You win a few. You lose a few. Some are rained out. But you got to dress for all of them."

One of life's great challenges is showing up consistently, even when you don't want to. As Dave Roberts, the manager of the Dodgers says, "The best ability is availability." Be accountable, follow through, be true to your word, take the responsibility that's yours, and be willing to fail.

The interesting thing about baseball is how humbling it is. Great hitters only hit the ball, reaching base safely, one third of the time. They *fail* two thirds of the time. Average hitters hit safely only one fourth of the time. They *fail* three out of four times. Yet they go to the plate over and over again.

Persistence, relentlessness, and ferocity are great qualities. They propel our best intentions. They are fuel for growth and success even in the face of unknown challenges.

Don Miguel Ruiz suggests in his fourth agreement, "Always do your best. Your best is going to change from moment to moment; it will be different when you are healthy as opposed to sick. Under any circumstance, simply do your best and you will avoid self-judgment, self-abuse, and regret."

What happens when you chop wood and carry water?

SWEET STUFF

UNDERSTANDING AND GRATITUDE

The Building Block Theory of Life

Henry Ford thought of experience as "the thing of supreme value" in life.

The Building Block Theory of Life expands on this notion. Throughout our lifetimes, we collect thousands upon thousands of experiences. Think of each experience as a block. After gathering a number of blocks, we build something. We may like what we built and keep it for a while. Or, as Robert Holden suggests by the title of his book, *Shift Happens*, we might tear it down, or perhaps someone else knocks it over and we are forced to build something new.

In either case, we are always acquiring new blocks!

I built my first career over thirty years. Then one day, everything changed and it collapsed. Thirty years gone in an instant. It was like experiencing a death—of my career, my livelihood, and my sense of ego identification. I went through Kübler-Ross's five stages of grief: denial, bargaining, anger, depression, and finally acceptance.

Although the structural edifice of my career had been knocked down, I still had all the blocks I had ever accumulated. So, once I got over myself (and I admit it took a while), I started to build something new. When you get right down to it, what choice do we have?

What are you building?

SWEET STUFF

UNDERSTANDING AND GRATITUDE

Once you know what peace is, you know what it isn't.

Peace and serenity are not the absence of conflict but instead the ability to deal with it. Pause when agitated. "Be still and know."—Psalm 46:10

How can we learn to turn chaos, difficulty, and failure into growth opportunities that lead to a more peaceful existence? How can we learn to do less and *be* more?

Perhaps this is a life passage, a stage for older folks. But I can't help but wonder how much better my youth would have been had I been able to find some peace within, had I been able to appreciate the moment and the beauty surrounding me instead of running from the past or chasing the future.

At times I find myself feeling bad that I feel so good. Things might be crumbling around me and yet I, in the eye of the hurricane, can often find quiet and peace.

"Ninety percent of life is letting go and the other half is being quiet."—Anonymous

Where do you find peace?

SWEET STUFF

UNDERSTANDING AND GRATITUDE

Have nothing to defend.

We are so compelled to defend. We defend our identity, our ideas, our personhood, our religion, our politics, and everything else that we think of as "ours." So much of what we defend feels crucial to our very existence, to our being and doing in the world.

What if we don't have to defend any of it? Obviously, we must defend when there is an actual real-world threat. But these real-world threats rarely come.

The threats I'm referring to are the illusory threats, the threats we perceive to our egos, beliefs, and self-images. What if we don't have to attend every argument we were invited to? What would it be like to feel so secure in our ownness, that we didn't feel the need to argue, protect, or explain anything? What if there was nothing to defend?

What would it be like to live free of fear?

SWEET STUFF

UNDERSTANDING AND GRATITUDE

"'No' is a complete sentence."
—Anne Lamott

This little two-letter puppy is one of the most necessary and scary words in the English language. "No" is an absolute. It's definitive. It's important, and yet it can also feel selfish, cruel, and scary.

I would often worry that if I told people "no," they wouldn't love me anymore. I was afraid of being rejected and, even worse, *abandoned*. This fear was often stronger than my desire to tell the truth.

Saying "no" felt horrible as I looked in your eyes and saw your disappointment and hurt. It's such a little word but it seemed to threaten my security. So, of course I would say "yes" and then resent you for making me do something I didn't want to do. Or resent myself for being so easily manipulated by my own fears. Or instead of "yes" or "no," I might say "maybe" or "perhaps" or "we'll see"—which only kicked the can down the road.

"No" is a boundary. It's crucial to harmonious living. Both "yes" and "no" are critical indicators of who we are, what we need, and what we want or don't want. When we can speak with true conviction, we know who we are. When we can't, we are a mystery to ourselves and to others.

What is the power of "no" in your life?

SWEET STUFF

UNDERSTANDING AND GRATITUDE

"The highest form of wisdom is kindness."
—*The Talmud*

Aesop said, "No act of kindness, no matter how small, is ever wasted."

My eldest son, age twenty-five, suffered with mental illness his whole short life. One day, we were headed to acupuncture. It helped calm us both. As we exited the freeway onto the off-ramp, we noticed a young man about my son's age on the corner begging for money. We passed him and turned left. My son shouted, "Stop, stop!" I pulled over and stopped. He said, "Give me twenty dollars!" I suspected what he wanted so I gave him ten instead.

He got out of the car and ran back to the corner where the young man waited. I watched them in the rear-view mirror. I watched them talking. I watched my son give him the money. I watched them hug in a deep embrace as if holding onto life itself and then I watched my son run back to the car. He jumped in, shut the door, looked right at me and said, "If it weren't for you and Mommy, that would be me."

I pulled back into traffic and we went to acupuncture.

What does kindness cost?

SWEET STUFF

UNDERSTANDING AND GRATITUDE

> "Do I contradict myself?
> Very well then, I contradict myself.
> I am large. I contain multitudes."
> —Walt Whitman

This idea of "containing multitudes" is so profoundly magnanimous. It forgives all our human contradictions. All our many paradoxes, varying emotions, crazy thoughts, our trials and tribulations, ups and downs, and everything else in this wonderful crazy life of ours.

It holds and affirms all our humanity, our failures and successes, our knowing and unknowing, and our frailties and strengths. It forgives our poverty of spirit and alludes to all the great things that make each of us the person we are: creative, resourceful, and whole.

As Rainer Maria Rilke said, "Be patient toward all that is unsolved in your heart and try to love the questions themselves."

What wonderful contradictions make you who you are?

SWEET STUFF

UNDERSTANDING AND GRATITUDE

> "A person needs three things
> to be truly happy in this world:
> someone to love, something to do,
> and something to hope for."
> —Tom Bodett

Simple and straightforward; Tom Bodett presents three life fulfillments with real resonance and value.

When I feel wanting or disconnected, it's usually because I am overwhelmed or distracted. Things of real value become obscured by other stuff of less importance.

Steven Covey suggests in the four quadrants of his Time Management Matrix that we are so busy managing or avoiding the urgent and/or unimportant that we fail to concentrate enough time on preparing, focusing, planning, prevention, values clarification, self-care, relationship building, and true recreation/relaxation.

If we did, our experience would change.

Where is your focus?

SWEET STUFF

UNDERSTANDING AND GRATITUDE

Surrender is a winning proposition.

My peace of mind is directly proportional to my willingness to surrender my will to something greater than myself.

I used to think that I was in charge. I was deluded by a sense of self-importance about my own impact. I went to college, I was relatively on the ball, and I was successful in my chosen career. Controller, fixer, problem solver, creator, developer—hell, I could manage my world just fine, and even yours, time permitting.

But at what cost? And could I really? It turned out that all my manipulations took their toll, chasing around trying to make everything work and everyone happy. I couldn't keep up. The task I assigned myself was impossible. Often frustrated and demoralized, I would trip and fall. "Nothing's going my way, what can I do?"

It turns out that the flow of life is eminently capable of getting along without us. Stop struggling with that which you can't control. Surrender. If it's out of your hands, get it out of your mind.

What do you notice when you let it be?

SWEET STUFF

UNDERSTANDING AND GRATITUDE

I am before the thought.

Well, here we are again, right back where we started, talking about thought. Just another example of how thought goes 'round and 'round in constant unrelenting conversations with itself.

Smart folks tell me there is a "me" that precedes my thoughts—a me before mind—a "me mystery." I often wonder if seeking this "me" might be the essence of my life journey.

Who is this "me" that is without thought? What is this "me" that transcends my body, my mind, and my circumstances? Perhaps this "me" is pure spirit, the intrinsic internal hum that elevates my days.

It's hard to assign a value to this "me" because it's so ethereal and translucent, so non-quantifiable, so non-monetizable, except when I slow down and listen. *Then it's worth everything!*

These are the times when heaven whispers.

What does it feel like, this grace within?

CHAPTER 9

More Thinking About Thinking by Great Thinkers

MORE THINKING ABOUT THINKING

"The outer world, far from being the prison of circumstances that we commonly supposed it to be, has actually no character whatsoever of its own, either good or bad. It has only the character that we give it by our own thinking. . . We can choose the sort of thoughts that we entertain. . . In point of fact, we always do. . . We have free will, but our free will lies in our choice of thought."
Emmet Fox, *The Sermon on the Mount*

"The first law of perception is you see what you want to see. Your eyes do the seeing, but it is your mind that decides what you focus on. In other words, you see what your mind is looking for. In effect you never see the world; you see your thoughts! This realization alone is a great key to personal alchemy and success. Perception is projection."
Robert Holden PhD, *Shift Happens*

MORE THINKING ABOUT THINKING

"Most people are so completely identified with the voice in the head — the incessant stream of involuntary and compulsive thinking and the emotions that accompany it — that we may describe them as being possessed by their mind. As long as you are completely unaware of this, you take the thinker to be who you are..."
Eckhart Tolle, *A New Earth*

"The bottom line is undeniable: If somehow the voice managed to manifest in a body outside of you, and you had to take it with you everywhere you went, you wouldn't last a day. If someone were to ask you what your new friend is like, you'd say, 'This is one seriously disturbed person. Just look up neurosis in the dictionary and you'll get the picture.'"
Michael A. Singer, *The Untethered Soul*

MORE THINKING ABOUT THINKING

"Life is cyclic in nature. Like a wheel, life goes round and round; sometimes we are on top of the wheel, sometimes we are on the bottom of it, but how we see these rotations determines how we are affected by them. We either perceive ourselves as victims and feel at the mercy of life's ups and downs or we move into *observer consciousness* and *witness* life as a reflection of our own mind."
Lynne Forrest, *Guiding Principles for Life Beyond Victim Consciousness* page 3

"The great Law of the Universe is that what you think in your mind you will produce in your experience. *As within, so without.* You cannot think one thing and produce another. If you want to control your circumstances for harmony and happiness then you must first control your thoughts for harmony and happiness, and then the outer things will follow."
Emmet Fox, *Sermon on the Mount* page 31

MORE THINKING ABOUT THINKING

"As long as we are too much locked in our own self-image, we are blind to the truth of who we are. Something brought us here in this environment intensely focused on looking at what we are not and trying to see what we are. I put that to be the most auspicious discovery possible in the human kingdom. A human being awake."
Moogi

"…When the tyrannical influence of the compensatory mind is temporarily lifted, a window is opened into un-integration. Then, like a child who is not afraid to be left alone, we are free to have a new experience. It is a paradox of self-discovery that we can know ourselves only by surrendering into the void."
Mark Epstein, MD, *Going to Pieces Without Falling Apart*

Photo by Katie Jackson

Art Dielhenn

Art is a certified career coach living in Los Angeles. In 1999 he founded Los Angeles Coaching to work with creative professionals and those in correlated industries who want to build sustainable thriving careers. Prior to coaching, he enjoyed a fulfilling, three-decade career as an A-list director of both public and commercial television.

Much of this book is graced by the thoughts, ideas, and writings of others. It's a synthesis of whatever Art has learned, picked up, or been gifted over the years. He has tried to give credit where credit is due. Any omissions were unintentional and the result of not being able to track down and credit the worthy source.

The library and quote tracker will highlight the authors so instrumental in the formation of this book.

Photo by Katie Jackson

Clemmy Le Busque

Clemmy is an artist and designer living in Los Angeles. Twenty-five years of failed psychotherapy suggests that Le Busque long ago gave up trying to work out the meaning of life through art.

The author of two graphic memoirs, in addition to the hilarious *Call Centre Diaries,* they hold an MA in Creative Writing and New Media and a BA in Fine Arts. When not working their day job as a drug and alcohol counselor, Le Busque is a keen student of nonviolent communication and a hypnotist.

Thanks

Al Watt, Rick Carson, Mindi White, Kat Chezum, Natasa Denman, Vivienne Mason, Julie Fisher, Isabelle Russell, Jack Grapes, Lynn Steinberg, PhD, Lynne Friedman-Gell, PhD, Anthony Lopez, MT, John Johns, Sarah Payne Stuart, John Steller, Ian Reed, Mike Olivas, Michael Topp, George Hartlaub, MD, Anna Delury, Liz Dubelman, Jesse Kanner, The SOMers, Jane Dystel, Miriam Goderich, Juan Moscoso, CPCC, Andrea Shrednick, PhD, Nikola Boskovski, Velin Saramov, my family, and all those friends, writers, thinkers, therapists, coaches, speakers, sharers, teachers and others who have helped elevate my consciousness above the level of Portobello Mushroom.

Library

Taming Your Gremlin, Rick Carson

A Master Class in Gremlin-Taming, Rick Carson

Guiding Principles for Life Beyond Victim Consciousness, Lynne Forrest

Conjoint Family Therapy, Virginia Satir

Introduction to the Internal Family Systems Model, Richard Schwartz, PhD

Going to Pieces Without Falling Apart, Mark Epstein, MD

The Power of Now, Eckhart Tolle

The New Earth, Eckhart Tolle

Merton's Palace of Nowhere, James Finley

The Contemplative Heart, James Finley

Shift Happens, Robert Holden, PhD

Alcoholics Anonymous, AA World Services

Twelve Steps and Twelve Traditions, AA World Services

The Untethered Soul, Michael A. Singer

Who Moved My Cheese? Spencer Johnson, MD

The Sermon on the Mount, Emmet Fox

The Little Red Book, Hazelden Foundation

The Tipping Point and *Blink*, Malcolm Gladwell

LIBRARY

Paths To Recovery, Al-Anon Family Groups

Opening Our Hearts, Transforming Our Losses, Al-Anon Family Groups

It's OK That You're Not OK, Megan Devine

Quiet, Susan Cain

Night Falls Fast, Kay Redfield Jamison

On Death and Dying, Elizabeth Kübler-Ross, MD

Life Strategies, Philip McGraw, PhD

Self Matters, Philip McGraw, PhD

*The Subtle Art of Not Giving a F*ck*, Mark Manson

Dreams Into Action, Milton Katselas

Practicing the Presence, Joel Goldstein

The Family Crucible, Augustus Y. Napier, PhD, and Carl Whitaker, MD

You're Not Crazy, Lynn Steinberg, PhD

Intimacy Anorexia, Douglas Weiss, PhD

Meditation For Beginners, Jack Kornfield

Developing The Leader Within You, John C. Maxwell

The Four Agreements, Don Miguel Ruiz

The Fifth Agreement, Don Miguel and Don Jose Ruiz

Mastery, George Leonard

Excuse Me, Your Life is Waiting, Lynn Grabhorn

Leadership and Self-Deception, Arbinger Institute

The Dark Night of the Soul, Gerald G. May, MD

Breathing Underwater, Richard Rohr

The Spirituality of Imperfection, Kurtz and Ketcham

Co-Active Coaching, Whitworth, Kimsey-House and Sandahl

The Coaching Connection, Gorrell and Hoover

KJV Study Bible, Barbour Publishing

Quotations Tracker

Thinking

United Negro College Fund, Pg. 19
Queen's Gazette, Pg. 19
Emo Philips, Pg. 23
Adyashanti, Pg. 23
Karen Lorre, Pg. 25
Spanish Proverb, Pg. 25
Wayne Dyer, Pg. 27
Eckhart Tolle, Pg. 29
Emmet Fox, Pg. 29
George R.R. Martin, Pg. 31
Eckhart Tolle, Pg. 31
Wayne Dyer, Pg. 33
Emmet Fox, Pg. 33
Diane Von Furstenberg, Pg. 35
Pema Chödrön, Pg. 37
Eckhart Tolle, Pg. 37

Talking and Listening

Mahatma Gandhi, Pg. 41
Iara Gassen, Pg. 43
Rumi, Pg. 43
Don Miguel Ruiz, Pg. 43
David Emerald, Pg. 45
Scott Howard, Pg. 45
Roni S. Lebauer, Pg. 47
Susan Cain, Pg. 51

QUOTATIONS TRACKER

Action and Achievement
Jerry Sternen, Pg. 55
Oxford Languages, Pg. 57
Milton Katselas, Pg. 57
Kobe Bryant, Pg. 57
Mahatma Gandhi, Pg. 61
Sylvia Boorstein, Pg. 67
Blaise Pascal, Pg. 67
Ice Cube, Pg. 69
National Center for Biotechnology Information (HALT), Pg. 69
George Doran, Arthur Miller & James Cunningham (S.M.A.R.T.), Pg. 75

The Challenging Stuff
Herodotus, Pg. 77

Ego, Control, and Attachment
Ken Blanchard, Pg. 81
Groucho Marx, Pg. 81
Rick Carson, Pg. 81
Arthur Rubenstein, Pg. 83
Buddha, Pg. 85
Eckhart Tolle, Pg. 85
Emmet Fox, Pg. 87
Anais Nin, Pg. 89
Epictetus, Pg. 89
Don Miguel Ruiz, Pg. 91
Oscar Wilde, Pg. 93
Werner Erhard, Pg. 97

Judgment, Blame, and Resentment
Eleanor Roosevelt, Pg. 111
Don Miguel Ruiz, Pg. 111
Anne Lamott, Pg. 113
St. Augustine, Pg. 115
Emmet Fox, Pg. 115
Bill Wilson, Pg. 117
Thomas Merton, Pg. 119
William Shakespeare, Pg. 119
Socrates, Pg. 119

Fear, Pain, and Worry
Georgia O'Keeffe, Pg. 123
Hakim Sanai, Pg. 125
Erma Bombeck, Pg. 127
Leo Buscaglia, Pg. 129
Richard Rohr, Pg. 131
Charles Eads, Pg. 131
Abraham Lincoln, Pg. 133
Dolly Parton, Pg. 135
The Little Red Book (Hazelden Foundation), Pg. 135
Maya Angelou, Pg. 135
Eleanor Roosevelt, Pg. 137

QUOTATIONS TRACKER

Past, Present, and Future
Dale Carnegie, Pg. 141
Robert Half, Pg. 143
Eleanor Roosevelt, Pg. 143
Kay Lyons, Pg. 143
Robert Hastings, Pg. 143
Doris Roberts, Pg. 143
Abraham Lincoln, Pg. 143

Relationship and Forgiveness
Desmond Tutu, Pg. 147
Louise L. Hay, Pg. 153
Dennis Merritt Jones, Pg. 153
Kahlil Gibran, Pg. 155
Richard Rohr, Pg. 159
Emmet Fox, Pg. 161

Humility and Acceptance
Graham Greene, Pg. 165
William Shakespeare, Pg. 169
Jon Kabat-Zinn, Pg. 171
The Shirelles, Pg. 173
Ralph Nader, Pg. 175
Mark Manson, Pg. 177
Mark Epstein, Pg. 179

Sweet Stuff
Emmet Fox, Pg. 188

Spirit and Awareness
Eleanor Roosevelt, Pg. 191
Apollon Maykov, Pg. 193
Megan Devine, Pg. 193
James Finley, Pg. 199
Jack Kornfield, Pg. 201

Understanding and Gratitude
Benjamin Franklin, Pg. 205
Mokokoma Mokhonoana, Pg. 205
Co-Active Coaching (Henry Kimsey-House, Laura Whitworth, and Phillip Sandahl), Pg. 209
Lao Tzu, Pg. 211
La Veneno, Pg. 213
George Meredith, Pg. 215
Alcoholics Anonymous, Pg. 215
German Proverb, Pg. 215
English Proverb, Pg. 219
Helen Keller, Pg. 219
Renuka Pitre, Pg. 219
Oscar Wilde, Pg. 221
George Carlin, Pg. 223
Doris Day, Pg. 225
Alan Alda, Pg. 227
Babe Ruth, Pg. 229
Satchel Paige, Pg. 229
Dave Roberts, Pg. 229

QUOTATIONS TRACKER

Don Miguel Ruiz, Pg. 229
Henry Ford, Pg. 231
Anne Lamott, Pg. 237
The Talmud, Pg. 239
Aesop, Pg. 239
Walt Whitman, Pg. 241
Rainer Maria Rilke, Pg. 241
Tom Bodett, Pg. 243
Steven Covey, Pg. 243

More Thinking about Thinking by Great Thinkers
Emmet Fox, Pg. 250
Robert Holden, Pg. 250
Eckhart Tolle, Pg. 251
Michael A. Singer, Pg. 251
Lynne Forrest, Pg. 252
Emmet Fox, Pg. 252
Mooji, Pg. 253
Mark Epstein, Pg. 253

Notes

NOTES

NOTES

NOTES

NOTES

www.ingramcontent.com/pod-product-compliance
Lightning Source LLC
Chambersburg PA
CBHW030255100526
44590CB00012B/408